W9-BYA-517

Sewn Toy Tales

Sewn Toy Tales

12 fun characters to make and love

David and Charles

www.rucraft.co.uk

A DAVID & CHARLES BOOK
Copyright © David & Charles Limited 2010

David & Charles is an F+W Media Inc. company
4700 East Galbraith Road, Cincinnati, OH 45236

First published in the UK and US in 2011

Text and designs copyright © Melly & Me 2011
Layout and photography copyright © David & Charles 2011

Melanie Hurlston and Rosalie Quinlan have asserted their right to be
identified as authors of this work in accordance with the Copyright,
Designs and Patents Act, 1988.

All rights reserved. No part of this publication may be reproduced,
stored in a retrieval system, or transmitted, in any form or by any
means, electronic or mechanical, by photocopying, recording or
otherwise, without prior permission in writing from the publisher.

Readers are permitted to reproduce any of the patterns or designs in
this book for their personal use and without the prior permission of
the publisher. However the designs in this book are copyright and
must not be reproduced for resale.

The author and publisher have made every effort to ensure that all
the instructions in the book are accurate and safe, and therefore
cannot accept liability for any resulting injury, damage or loss to
persons or property, however it may arise.

Names of manufacturers, fabric ranges and other products are
provided for the information of readers, with no intention to infringe
copyright or trademarks.

A catalogue record for this book is available from the British Library.

ISBN-13: 978-0-7153-3845-5 paperback
ISBN-10: 0-7153-3845-2 paperback

Printed in China by RR Donnelley
for David & Charles
Brunel House, Newton Abbot, Devon

Publisher Alison Myer
Acquisitions Editor Jennifer Fox-Proverbs
Assistant Editor Jeni Hennah
Project Editor Jo Richardson
Senior Designer Jodie Lystor
Photographer Lorna Yabsley
Senior Production Controller Kelly Smith

David & Charles publish high quality books on a wide range of subjects.
For more great book ideas visit: **www.rucraft.co.uk**

Contents

Introduction

When we were first approached by David & Charles to collaborate on a book of sewn toys, we were extremely excited and honoured. Imagine being given the opportunity to work with your sibling on a project that is guaranteed to generate so much pleasure and fulfilment. We had bundles of fun deciding which creatures we would best enjoy sharing with you.

As each creature came to life, we began to see the bigger picture and our excitement grew. When the day arrived to send our creations to the other side of the world, we were confident that they were going to be in the right hands, but we could never have envisaged just how wonderful the end result would be.

So now meet our magical collection of soft toy personalities, which you can easily re-create following the detailed step-by-step instructions. Close-up photos home in on the particular features – whether it's their ears, facial expressions or clothing – that give them their special individual character, so that you too can bring each creature to life. As well as templates for all the soft toys, the section at the back of the book advises you on the basic tools you'll need, choosing fabric to create the most exciting effects and the simple sewing techniques involved to achieve professional results.

We can be sure that as you make these creatures for yourself or your loved ones, they will bring you as much joy as they did us.

May the floss be with you!

Melly & Rosie

tilly the doll

Who's that striding around the place? Oh, we should have guessed – it's jolly Ms Tilly the dolly. She's an energetic, oudoorsy sort of gal, bounding along on those gangly long legs with her ponytails flying in the wind – and she's great fun and bubbly with it. But to be honest, her head is in the clouds in more than the literal sense.

Making Tilly, however, is a straightforward, down-to-earth business using standard soft toy-making and sewing techniques plus a little embroidery for her sweet rosy-cheeked face. And to finish off, you'll need to do some simple fabric painting for her shoes.

you will need

- 30cm x 50cm (12in x 20in) green patterned cotton fabric (body and upper arms)
- 25cm x 40cm (10in x 16in) pink striped cotton fabric (legs)
- 30cm x 50cm (12in x 20in) calico (arms and head)
- 30cm x 30cm (12in x 12in) small pink checked cotton fabric (hair)
- 25cm x 60cm (10in x 24in) yellow patterned cotton fabric (pantaloons)
- 15cm x 15cm (6in x 6in) fusible webbing
- Six-strand embroidery thread (floss): brown and pink
- Pink acrylic folk art paint
- Acrylic folk art matt varnish
- Basic tool kit (see pages 102–103)

Finished size: about 40cm (16in) tall

One Trace all the templates for Tilly from page 125 onto template plastic, transferring all the markings, and cut them out around the outside lines.

two Fold the green patterned fabric in half, right sides together. Draw around the body template once onto the folded fabric, **but don't cut out**, as this will be sewn before cutting out.

three Fold the pink striped fabric in half, right sides together. Draw around the leg template twice onto the folded fabric, ensuring that you line up the stripes accurately. **Don't cut out**, as these will be sewn before cutting out.

Tilly's characteristic lanky look is all in her legs, and the bold yet uniform stripy fabric really emphasizes her strongest feature, contrasting with the patterned pantaloons. Just make sure those stripes match up along the seams.

four For Tilly's arms, cut one strip of green patterned fabric measuring 5cm x 50cm (2in x 20in) and one strip of calico measuring 13cm x 50cm (5in x 20in). Sew the green strip to the top of the calico strip along the 50cm (20in) edge. Open out and press.

five Fold the fabric panel for the arm in half, right sides together, so that the fabrics meet each other horizontally. Press. Draw around the arm template twice onto the folded fabric panel, ensuring that you line up the sleeve line on the template with the green fabric. **Don't cut out**, as these will be sewn before cutting out.

six Cut a piece of calico measuring 15cm x 13cm (6in x 5in). Draw around Tilly's head template onto the wrong side of the single fabric. Flip the calico piece over and place, drawn-side down, on a light box or against a sunny window. Using a light grey lead pencil, draw the head shape onto the right side of the fabric, ensuring that it lines up exactly with the drawing on the wrong side of the fabric. This is done so that you can accurately position Tilly's wig piece overlay.

seven Draw around Tilly's wig piece onto the paper side of the fusible webbing. Cut two pieces of pink checked fabric measuring 15in x 13in (6in x 5in). Iron the fusible webbing to the wrong side of one fabric piece. Cut out the wig piece overlay on the solid (not dotted) outside line.

eight Remove the paper backing and position the wig piece carefully over the right side of Tilly's head panel, using your pencil drawing to help you accurately position the hair over the face area. Press to fuse the two fabrics together. Hand backstitch or blanket stitch (see pages 106–107) (or machine stitch using a tight zigzag stitch) the inside edge of Tilly's hair.

nine Place the other piece of pink checked fabric, right sides together, on the front of Tilly's head panel. Sew Tilly's head together along the outside line that you had previously marked, **but don't leave a turning gap**.

ten Cut Tilly's head out 6mm (¼in) outside the stitched line. Cut a small slit in the **back only (pink fabric side)** of Tilly's head, positioned horizontally at the centre bottom, approximately 1.25cm (½in) up from the stitched line. Turn the head right side out through the small slit.

eleven Stuff the head firmly with toy filling (see page 110) and then overstitch the opening closed at the back of the head.

twelve Machine stitch the body and legs along the marked outside lines, leaving the ends open for turning. Machine stitch the arms together along the marked outside line, leaving the gap open for turning as on the template.

thirteen Cut out the body, legs and arms approximately 6mm (¼in) outside the stitched lines. Turn right sides out.

fourteen Stuff the arms firmly with toy filling and ladder stitch the openings closed (see page 112). Stuff the legs firmly to the fill line. Machine sew across the fill line, leaving the tops of the legs empty. Following the Inserting Legs technique on page 113, insert the legs. Stuff the body firmly with toy filling and ladder stitch the opening between the legs closed.

fifteen Take the body and place the head over the top of the body, overlapping the stuffing slit in the head. Following the Attaching Parts with Ladder Stitch technique on page 115, ladder stitch the head onto the body where indicated on the body template, right around the seam line of the top of the body. This stitching should cover the stuffing slit and keep the head firmly in place.

sixteen Ladder stitch the top 1.75cm (¾in) of each arm to the side of Tilly's body.

Tip

You can add an extra dimension of personality by attaching Tilly's head to her body at a slight angle.

Instead of conventional doll's hair, Tilly has an eccentric pink checked wig as befits her character – another way in which she stands out from the crowd. Note where the separate stuffed ponytails are attached.

Tilly's long, slender arms add to her animated appearance, and they cleverly incorporate her blouse sleeve, the patterned fabric being sewn to the calico before cutting out. See here where her arms are ladder stitched to her body.

seventeen Using a vanishing marker, draw the eyes, mouth and cheeks onto Tilly's face. Use three strands of brown embroidery thread (floss) to embroider the eyes using satin stitch (see page 107). Using three strands of pink embroidery thread (floss), embroider the cheeks with running stitch and the mouth with backstitch (see page 106) – you should be able to hide the knot behind Tilly's head, in between her head and her body.

eighteen Draw around the ponytail template twice onto the remaining pink checked fabric folded in half. Sew along the drawn lines, leaving the ends open. Cut out each ponytail 6mm (¼in) outside the stitched outline. Clip the curves and turn right sides out.

nineteen Stuff each ponytail with toy filling. Turn the ends under by 6mm (¼in) and ladder stitch the ponytail into position on Tilly's head (see page 115), making sure that you line up each ponytail with the bottom of Tilly's hairline.

TILLY'S CLOTHES AND SHOES

one Draw around the pantaloon template onto the yellow patterned fabric folded in half and cut out on the drawn line. Machine stitch the two pantaloon pieces together along both the crotch seam lines as marked on the template, taking a 6mm (¼in) seam. Pull the seams to the front and back and machine stitch up one leg and then down the other.

two Turn the waist and leg bottoms under by 1.25cm (½in) and press. Using six strands of pink embroidery thread (floss), hand sew medium running stitches along the edge of the waist, without securing the thread at the end. Place the pantaloons on Tilly, pull the unsecured thread end to gather up the fabric evenly and tie securely in a knot. Sew the pantaloons to Tilly's body by taking the thread through her body and out the back of the pantaloons, then back through to the front before tying in a knot.

three Gather the leg bottoms in the same way, sewing them to the legs as in the previous step so that they remain at the same level.

four Using your lead pencil, draw the shoe line onto Tilly's feet as marked on the template. Paint and then varnish the shoes following the Painting on Fabric technique on page 115.

Wearing pantaloons rather than a frock means that Tilly is suitably clad for any adventure she fancies – the trouser hems are sewn to her legs to keep them securely in place. And she's wearing go-anywhere shoes.

harry the monster

When Harry's around, be warned – this monster's a mean party animal. Which is not hard to imagine looking at his outrageously adorned body, studded with bright orange discs and 'tattooed' with white kisses. That's if you've managed to get over the shock of this crazy guy's eyes on stalks, horns-for-arms and snaking mouth. And then there's the mad bright orange dreadlocks-with-a-difference.

As the construction of Harry's body is so quick and easy, your time is freed up to go to town on his appliquéd and embroidered body decoration, to give him his unique zany character.

you will need

- 40cm x 60cm (16in x 24in) blue felted wool fabric (main body)
- 20cm x 20cm (8in x 8in) orange felted wool fabric (appliquéd circles)
- 5cm x 10cm (2in x 4in) white felted wool fabric (outer eyes)
- 5cm x 10cm (2in x 4in) black felted wool fabric (pupils)
- 7cm x 25cm (2¾in x 10in) red felted wool fabric (horns)
- Six-strand embroidery thread (floss): lime green, purple, red, yellow, white, black, orange
- Plastic-coated freezer paper
- Thin permanent marker
- Large-eyed needle
- Basic tool kit (see pages 102–103)

Finished size: about 35cm (13¾in) tall

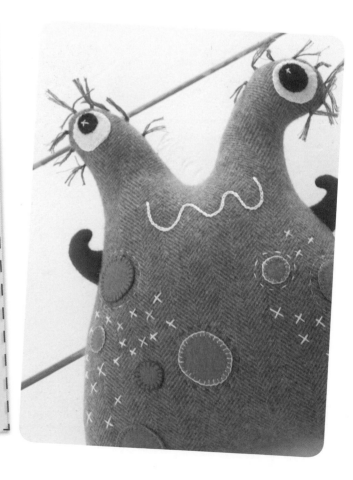

one Trace all the templates for Harry, including the large and small body circles and outer eyes and pupils, from page 120 onto template plastic, transferring any markings. Cut them out around the outside lines.

two Draw around the body template onto the paper side of the freezer paper. Flip the template and draw a second body onto the same side of the freezer paper. Cut out both body pieces along the drawn lines.

three Cut the blue felted wool fabric in half so that you have two pieces each measuring 40cm x 30cm (16in x 12in).

four Iron the plastic side of the second freezer paper template to the centre of one of your blue felted wool fabric pieces on the wrong side of the fabric. Draw around the freezer paper template with a thin permanent marker (you will use this line to sew on later). Mark the turning gap, as indicated on the template.

five Iron the first freezer paper template to the right side of the same piece of blue felted wool fabric, making sure that you line it up in exactly the same position as the freezer paper on the back of the fabric.

six Draw around the front template, using white tailor's chalk – this is to ensure that you have an accurate outline in order to correctly position the appliqué pieces. Remove the freezer paper from both the front and back of your piece of felted wool fabric.

seven Use the circle templates to cut out four large and five small circles from the orange felted wool fabric. Position the circles as indicated on the body template. Pin the circles carefully in place on Harry's front body

eight Using six strands of embroidery thread (floss), blanket stitch around each circle, alternating between lime green, purple, red and yellow (see page 107).

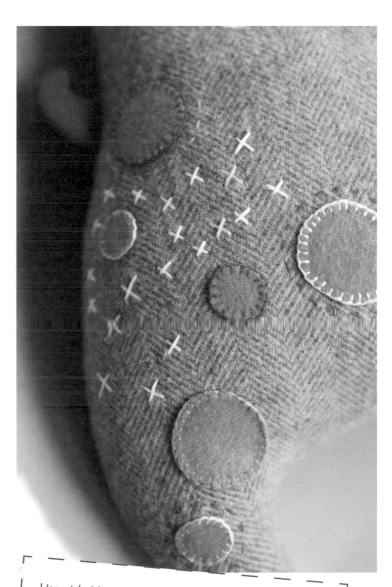

Harry's boldly embellished body speaks volumes about his extrovert, creative nature. It may look impressive, but it's easy to achieve using cut-out circles and basic embroidery stitches in contrasting thread.

nine Use the templates to cut out the two outer eyes from white felted wool fabric and the two pupils from black felted wool fabric. Position the outer eyes on Harry's front body and blanket stitch in place around the edges using six strands of white embroidery thread (floss). Position the pupils in place and hand stitch in the same way using black embroidery thread (floss).

ten Using the tailor's chalk, mark the mouth, the cross stitches and the running-stitch circles on Harry's front body. Using six strands of white embroidery thread (floss), work the mouth in chain stitch, stitch most of the cross stitches and sew a small cross stitch in the upper part of each pupil (see pages 106–107).

eleven Stitch the remainder of the cross stitches using lime green embroidery thread (floss). Work the running-stitch circles with red, yellow and white thread (floss), again using all six strands (see page 107). Put aside.

twelve Draw around the horn template twice onto the paper side of the freezer paper. Cut out both horn pieces along the drawn lines.

thirteen Fold the red felted wool fabric in half. Iron the plastic side of each of the horn freezer paper templates to the folded fabric, ensuring that they are spaced at least 1.25cm (½in) apart.

A smile doesn't come more wicked than this, does it? Working it using the whole six strands of the embroidery thread (floss) in chain stitch gives it full impact against the blue of the body fabric.

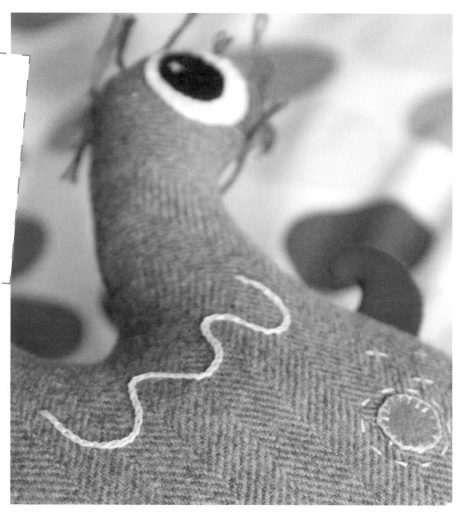

fourteen Leaving the freezer paper in position, machine stitch around the edge of each horn, leaving the ends open. Remove the freezer paper. Cut out each horn 6mm (¼in) outside the sewn lines. Turn the horns right sides out and press.

Tip

Harry will take a lot more stuffing than you think, as woollen fabric has a tendency to stretch.

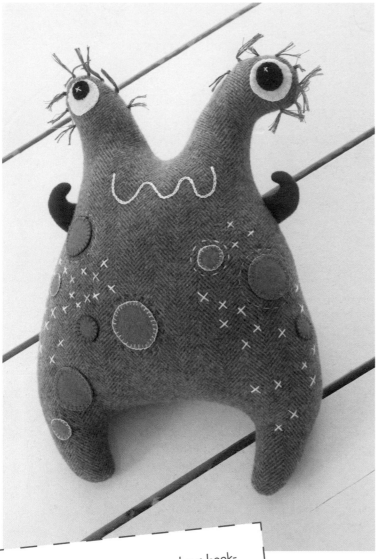

Who needs arms when you can have hook-like horns instead! They are cut from an appropriately devilish-looking flaming red felted wool fabric.

fifteen Place the front and back body panels right sides together. Using your permanent marker outline as a guide, cut the body shape out through both thicknesses of fabric 1.25cm (½in) outside the marked outline. Before stitching, position the horns where marked on the template between the front and back body pieces, with them pointing upwards and placed so that their raw open ends meet the raw edges of the body fabric.

sixteen Sew together along the marked outline, remembering to leave the turning gap as indicated on the template open. Clip slightly at all the curves, making sure not to cut too close to or into your seam.

seventeen Turn Harry right side out through the turning gap, then stuff him firmly with toy filling (see pages 110). Ladder stitch the opening closed (see page 112).

eighteen Thread a large-eyed needle with a double length of all six strands of orange embroidery thread (floss). Take a small stitch either side of the seam line at the top of one of Harry's eye stalks. Tie the thread in a tight reef (square) knot (see page 109) and trim the ends to approximately 2.5cm (1in) in length to create 'hair'.

nineteen Repeat the previous step along the seam line until you have the desired amount of hair. Add hair in the same way to the top of Harry's other eye stalk.

Harry's hair is as wild as his personality. But it's simply created by sewing on and then tying 12-strand lengths of embroidery thread (floss) and trimming to length. It's so cutting edge a hairstyle, it could catch on!

alexander the caterpillar

Here he comes – although he could be some time arriving – dear old Alexander the Caterpillar, wriggling along on his stout body/leg segments, which are alternated with eye-catching patterned yo-yos, and peering about trying to remember where he's going. A trifle confused he may be as well as a bit slow-moving, but he's nonetheless handsome as bugs go.

Besides the routine cutting out, sewing and stuffing of pattern pieces, the making of Alexander involves a simple hand-gathering technique to create the yo-yos from fabric circles, which are then threaded together with the body/leg sections in a set sequence.

you will need

- 40cm (16in) x the full width of green spotted fabric (body/leg sections and head)
- 30cm x 30cm (12in x 12in) purple fabric (antennae and nose)
- Scraps of white and black wool felt (eyes)
- 15 random patterned fabric circles, cut using the large yo-yo template on page 120
- 1 small patterned fabric circle, cut using the small yo-yo template on page 120
- Scraps of fusible webbing
- Six-strand embroidery thread (floss): white, black, red
- Large sailmaker's needle (with a very large eye)
- 3m (3⅓yd) of 6mm (¼in) cotton twill tape
- Basic tool kit (see pages 102–103)

Finished size: about 40cm (16in) long x 15cm (6in) tall

ONE Trace the body/leg section, head, outer eye, pupil, nose and antenna templates for Alexander from page 120 onto template plastic, transferring all the markings, and cut them out around the outside lines.

two Fold the green spotted fabric in half. Draw around the body/leg section template six times and the head template once onto the folded fabric. **Don't cut out**, as these will be sewn before cutting out.

three Fold the purple fabric in half. Draw around the antenna twice and the nose once onto the folded fabric. **Don't cut out**, as these will be sewn before cutting out.

You'd think with his big, curly antennae to guide him that Alexander would always know where he was going, but I think he's lost again. Still, they look the part – if you stuff them firmly enough, that is.

four Iron fusible webbing to the wrong side of your white and black wool felt scraps. Draw round the outer eye and pupil templates twice each and cut out on the drawn lines.

five Machine stitch all the body/leg sections together around the marked lines, but **don't leave a turning gap**. Stitch the head pieces together in the same way, but again, **don't leave a turning gap**.

six Sew the antennae pieces together along the drawn lines, leaving the ends open. Sew the nose pieces together, but **don't leave a turning gap**.

seven Cut out all the shapes approximately 6mm (¼in) outside the stitched lines. Cut a turning slit through **one layer only** of each body/leg section, the head and the nose where indicated on the templates. Turn all the pieces right sides out through the turning slits.

Tip

The stitching of the turning slits to close doesn't need to be especially neat, as you won't see it, but make sure it's good and strong.

eight Stuff the body/leg sections firmly with toy filling (see pages 110), then ladder stitch the turning slits closed (see page 112). Stuff the head and nose in the same way, stitching the turning slits closed.

nine Stuff the antennae firmly to the top opening. Turn the ends of the antennae in and stitch closed. Following the Attaching Parts with Ladder Stitch technique on page 115, sew the antennae to the top of the head, positioning as indicated on the head template.

'Follow me'

ten Ladder stitch the nose in position on the front of the head, so that the turning slit is hidden against the head – it must be ladder stitched all along the nose seam line.

eleven Attach the outer eyes and pupils to the head by peeling off the paper backing and ironing into position. Using two strands of white embroidery thread (floss), blanket stitch the outer eyes around the edges to secure (see page 107). Repeat for the pupils using black embroidery thread (floss). Using two strands of red embroidery thread (floss), work the mouth in backstitch (see page 106).

twelve To make the yo-yos, lay a large fabric circle, right-side down, on your work surface. Fold the outer 6mm (¼in) edge of the fabric to the front. Hand sew medium running stitches around the outer edge, without securing the thread at the end (see page 106). Pull the unsecured thread end to gather up the fabric evenly, then tie in a secure knot (see the diagrams below). Repeat with the remaining 14 large fabric circles and the small fabric circle.

Poor old Alexander, he does look puzzled doesn't he. His expression is cleverly conveyed by the offset positioning of his mouth, easily embroidered in backstitch.

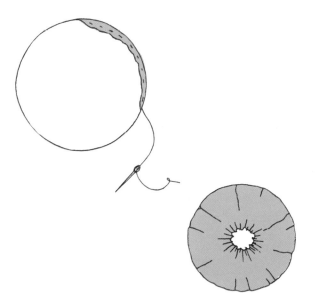

thirteen Using a vanishing marker, mark the threading markers on the body/leg sections, as indicated on the template, which is where the cotton twill tape will be threaded through. Mark corresponding points on each of the 15 large yo-yos.

fourteen Using the large sailmaker's needle, thread the twill tape double through the first body/leg section at the right-hand side marker only. Now thread the twill tape through the right-hand side marker of three large yo-yos. Thread through the next body/leg section and then three more large yo-yos.

fifteen Continue to thread all the remaining body/leg sections and large yo-yos through the right-hand side threading markers.

sixteen When you have reached the end, thread the twill tape back through the left-hand markers of each body/leg section and yo-yo. Pull all the pieces together firmly and tie the ends of the twill tape together with a firm reef knot.

He might be a little slow in the movement department, but Alexander's body more than makes up for that with its flexibility. That's because his smart body/leg sections and interspersed gathered fabric circles are all ingeniously threaded together using cotton twill tape.

seventeen Ladder stitch the small yo-yo to the end of Alexander to cover the twill tape.

eighteen Ladder stitch Alexander's head in position at the other end of the body, covering the knot in the twill tape in the same process.

As Alexander's rear end may well be a long time in view as he slowly disappears into the sunset, it's adorned in style with a final fabric rosette, which actually also serves a practical purpose in concealing the tape end.

lou-lou
the panda

If you come quietly, you can meet Lou-Lou the Panda – she can be rather shy and awkward with strangers. But doesn't she look cute or daft depending on your point of view in her polka dot dress and spotted pantaloons – colour-coordinated to match her eye markings! She can also be a bit of a liability, to be honest, with her pigeon toes and banana-like arms – just try not to laugh at her too loudly.

After the usual soft toy-making and embroidery procedures, you can have fun here creating Lou-Lou's Sunday best outfit, using machine gathering to make her frock extra flouncy.

you will need

- 30cm (12in) x the full width pink woven wool fabric (body, legs and arms)
- 5cm x 10cm (2in x 4in) each of black, white and red wool felt (eyes and nose)
- 20cm (8in) x the full width of black and white small polka dot fabric (pinafore)
- 25cm x 50cm (10in x 20in) black and white large polka dot fabric (pantaloons)
- 10cm x 20cm (4in x 8in) fusible webbing
- Six-strand embroidery thread (floss): black, white, red
- Basic tool kit (see pages 102–103)

Finished size: about 40cm (16in) tall

one Trace all the templates for Lou-Lou, including the nose, outer and inner eye and pupil, from page 121 onto template plastic, transferring all the markings, and cut them out around the outside lines.

two Fold the pink fabric in half. Draw around the body template once, then the arm, leg and ear templates twice each on the folded fabric. **Don't cut out**, as these will be sewn before cutting out.

three Iron fusible webbing to the wrong side of your black, white and red wool felt pieces. Draw around the outer eye and pupil templates twice each onto the black felt. Do the same with the inner eye template and the white felt. Cut out on the drawn lines. Draw around the nose template once onto the red felt and cut out on the drawn line.

For someone so bashful, Lou-Lou is a sturdy young thing, with her chubby pink arms – but I guess they're all the better for hiding behind! They will need some firm stuffing, and of course the usual secure stitching to her body with strong polyester thread.

four Machine stitch the body pieces together by sewing around the marked line, leaving the bottom open. Sew the arms and legs in the same way, leaving the ends open for turning. Sew the ears along the drawn lines, leaving the turning gaps, as indicated on the template. Cut out all the shapes approximately 6mm (¼in) outside the stitched lines. Turn everything right sides out.

Now Lou-Lou's emerged from the undergrowth, she's sitting pretty on a designer chair that shows off her fetching outfit. To make things easy, the trick is to stuff her larger-than-life legs and sew them in place before stuffing her body.

five Stuff the legs firmly with toy filling until 2.5cm (1in) from the top opening (see page 110). Insert the legs into the body, following the Inserting Legs technique on page 113. Stuff the body firmly. Ladder stitch the opening between the legs closed (see page 112).

six Stuff the arms firmly to 2.5cm (1in) from the top opening. Turn the ends of the arms in and ladder stitch closed. Ladder stitch the arms to the side of the body, as indicated on the template.

seven Turn the raw ends of the ears in and stitch the opening closed. Ladder stitch the ears in position on Lou-Lou's head, as indicated on the template.

eight Position the eyes and nose, then attach them to Lou-Lou's head by peeling off the backing paper and ironing into position. Using two strands of black embroidery thread (floss), blanket stitch around the edges of the outer eyes to secure (see page 107). Repeat for the inner eyes, using white embroidery thread (floss), and then the pupils using black thread (floss). Sew a small cross stitch of white thread (floss) on the pupils (see page 107). Using two strands of red embroidery thread (floss), stitch the line under Lou-Lou's nose in backstitch and her mouth in satin stitch (see pages 106–107).

LOU-LOU'S CLOTHES

one Cut two rectangles of small polka dot fabric for the pinafore, each measuring 33cm x 18cm (13in x 7in).

two Fold the remaining small polka dot fabric in half, right sides together. Draw around the bodice template once onto the folded fabric.

three Set your sewing machine to the longest stitch and sew along the 33cm (13in) edge of one of the fabric rectangles, without securing the thread at the end. Pull the unsecured thread end to gather up the fabric evenly, enough to fit the bottom edge of one of the bodice pieces. Repeat with remaining fabric rectangle.

four Machine stitch each gathered rectangle separately to the bottom of each bodice piece, right sides together, taking a 6mm (¼in) seam. Open out and press.

Tip

Make sure that you place Lou-Lou's eye appliqués in a non-symmetrical way, to make her facial expression more convincing.

She does look rather dumbstruck (or plain dumb), doesn't she? This characterful expression is achieved by the combination of the down-turned appliquéd eyes and the embroidered line-and-dot mouth.

five Place one dress piece on top of the other, right sides together, and machine stitch from the top sleeve end to the neck markings on both sides, as indicated on the bodice template. Sew from the bottom sleeve end up the arm and down the side of the bodice. Continue sewing down the sides of the dress to the hem.

six Turn the bottom of the dress under 6mm (¼in) twice and press, then sew the hem in place. Turn the dress right side out and press. Turn the sleeve ends under 1.25cm (½in) and press.

seven Place the dress on Lou-Lou. Using six strands of embroidery thread (floss), hand sew medium running stitches around the neck, without securing the thread at the end (see page 108). Pull the unsecured thread end to gather up the fabric evenly and then tie off the thread to secure. Gather the sleeve ends in the same way.

eight Fold the large polka dot fabric in half. Draw around the pantaloons template once onto the folded fabric and cut out on the marked outside line.

Lou-Lou's girlie frock, hand-gathered at the neck and sleeves, is in comic contrast to her endearingly chunky, clumsy-looking limbs.

Tip

Take a stitch into the body to ensure that the pantaloons won't fall down!

nine Place the pantaloon pieces on top of each other, right sides together, and machine stitch together along both crotch seam lines. Bring the front and back seams together and sew together from the bottom of one leg up to the crotch and back down the other leg. Turn right side out and press. Turn the bottom of the pantaloons under 6mm (¼in) twice and press. Sew the hem in place.

ten Turn the waistband under 1.25cm (½in). Using strong thread, hand sew medium running stitches around the waistband, without securing the thread at the end. Place the pantaloons on Lou-Lou, pull up the unsecured thread to gather the fabric evenly and tie in a knot to secure.

To add to her slightly 'dotty' look, Lou-Lou's pantaloons are left loose and baggy, rather than gathered at the leg bottoms, so that they hang down below her dainty dress.

preston the lion

Gather round everybody, Preston the Lion is about to hold forth – at length, so make yourselves comfortable. His proportions are a bit of a giveaway: just look at the size of that head. But does that indicate big brain capacity or just big-headedness? A bit of both probably. And while he may be short in stature, Preston is big on tall tales. Note that he is also sitting down, meaning the telling could take some time.

There's button jointing of limbs to be done here, along with machine gathering for the mane and a little basic embroidery for the facial features and paws.

you will need

- 25cm (10in) x the full width of light brown gingham fabric (body)
- 15cm x 15cm (6in x 6in) contrast-patterned fabric (tummy and nose)
- 6.5cm (2½in) x the full width of orange fabric (mane and tail tip)
- Scrap of black wool felt or fabric (eyes)
- 10cm x 15cm (4in x 6in) fusible webbing
- Six-strand embroidery thread (floss): orange, black, white
- 2 large orange buttons, 2.5cm (1in) diameter
- 2 smaller orange buttons, 1.75cm (¾in) diameter
- Basic tool kit (see pages 102–103)

Finished size: about 25cm (10in) tall

Preston's smart mind is matched by his 'tailored' appearance. Choose a really good contrast of fabric for the tummy and nose, like the wacky tape-measure pattern used here, but with a linking element, such as the checked design in this case.

four Fold the tail fabric panel in half, right sides together, so that the fabrics meet each other horizontally. Press. Draw around the tail template onto the folded fabric, making sure that you match up the line marked on the template with the seam where the fabrics meet.

five Machine stitch the arms, legs and ears together along the drawn lines, leaving gaps for turning, as indicated on the templates. Sew the body together along the drawn line, but **don't leave a turning gap**. Sew the tail in the same way, but again **don't leave a turning gap**.

six **Without** sewing it together, cut the head out of the double fabric 6mm (¼in) outside the marked line. Cut out all the other pieces 6mm (¼in) outside the stitched lines.

seven Turn the arms, legs and ears right sides out through the turning gaps. For the body and tail, cut a turning slit through **one layer only**, in the position indicated on the templates, before turning right sides out.

eight Cut a strip of orange fabric measuring 6.5cm x 76cm (2½in x 30in). Fold the strip in half, right sides out, all the way along the length. Press. Unfold the strip and sew the short ends together to form a ring. Re-fold the ring, right side out.

one Trace all the templates for Preston, including his eye, nose and tummy, from page 124 onto template plastic, transferring all the markings, and cut them out around the outside lines.

two Fold the light brown gingham in half, right sides together. Draw around the body and head templates once each and the ear, arm and leg templates twice each onto the folded fabric. **Don't cut out**, as these will be sewn before cutting out.

three For Preston's tail, you will need to cut one strip of light brown gingham fabric measuring 10cm x 20cm (4in x 8in) and one strip of orange fabric measuring 6.5cm x 20cm (2½in x 8in). Machine stitch the orange strip to the top of the light brown strip along the 20cm (8in) edge. Open out and press.

No wonder Preston has command of an audience – just look at that large, imposing head framed by a machine-gathered ring of strongly contrasting fabric for his mane. But a tuft of embroidery thread 'hair' in the centre adds a softening touch.

nine Set your sewing machine to the longest stitch and sew around the double raw edge of the ring, without securing the thread at the end. Pull the unsecured thread end to gather up the fabric evenly so that the ring measures approximately 46cm (18in) in circumference.

ten Take the two head fabric pieces, mark the wrong side of the back piece with a 'B' for 'back' and set aside. With your front head piece right-side up, tack (baste) the ears into position as indicated on the template. Face the top of the ears in towards the centre, with the raw edges of the ears meeting the raw edges of the head fabric. Now place both head pieces on top of each other, right sides together, with the ears between the two layers.

eleven Carefully position the ring of orange fabric, sandwiching it between the two layers of the head. The raw edges of the ring should line up with the raw edges of the head fabric. Tack (baste) into position.

twelve Machine stitch around the marked line on your head fabric, capturing the ears and the mane as you go, but **don't leave a turning gap.**

thirteen Cut the turning slit, as indicated on the template, through the **back layer of the head only** (the layer marked 'B'). Turn the head right side out through the turning gap.

fourteen Stuff the head firmly with toy filling (see page 110) and ladder stitch the turning gap closed (see page 112). Stuff the arms, legs, body and tail firmly with toy filling, then sew all the turning gaps closed.

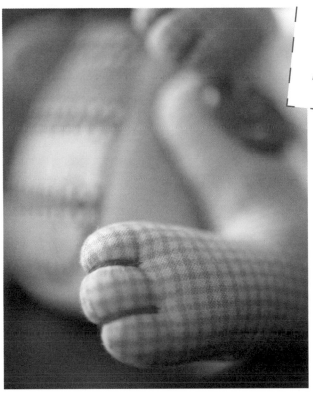

Our lion leader looks the part right down to the tips of his toes – well, paws actually! A little simple embroidery is all that's needed to create a convincing impression of the real thing.

One of Preston's defining features is his sharp-looking tummy patch, giving him an appropriate air of sartorial sophistication. A bold blanket-stitched edging adds the perfect finishing touch.

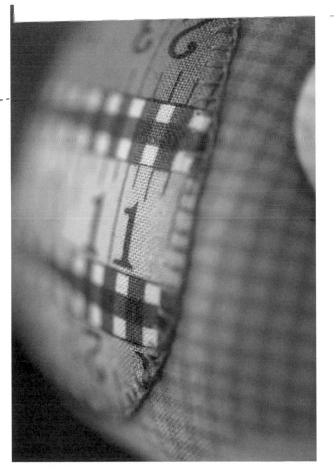

PRESTON'S DISTINGUISHING FEATURES

ONE Using six strands of orange embroidery thread (floss), take two large stitches through the ends of both legs and both arms to create 'paws'.

two Draw around the tummy and the nose templates once and the eye template twice onto the paper side of the fusible webbing. Cut out each shape 6mm (¼in) outside the drawn line.

Tip

Use the Sinking Knots technique on page 109 to start and finish the thread when sewing Preston's paws.

43

three Iron the tummy and nose to the back of the contrast fabric and the eyes to the back of the black wool felt or fabric. Cut out each shape. Remove the backing paper and position the tummy on the front of the body (the side with the turning slit). Press to fuse into position. Remove the backing paper from the nose and eyes and position them on the front of the head, as indicated on the template. Press to fuse them into position.

four Using two strands of embroidery (thread) floss in a matching colour, blanket stitch around the tummy, nose and the eyes (see page 107). Using white thread (floss), work a cross stitch on each eye, as indicated on the template (see page 107).

five Using 12 strands of orange embroidery thread (floss), make a small stitch at the top of Preston's head, right in the centre in front of the mane. Tie in reef (square) knot (see page 109) and trim the ends of the thread to approximately 2.5cm (1in) in length.

six Mark the mouth as indicated on the template with a vanishing marker. Use two strands of black embroidery thread (floss) to work in chain stitch (see page 106).

seven Place the head over the body so that both of the turning gaps meet. Following the Attaching Parts with Ladder Stitch technique on page 115, ladder stitch the head into position, sewing in a circle approximately 5cm (2in) in diameter around the neck seam.

eight Using the large buttons, join the legs to the sides of Preston's body, following the Button Jointing technique on page 114. Using the smaller buttons, join the arms to the sides of Preston's body in the same way.

He has a cool, steady, impersonal gaze does our lecturer Preston, which is just the expression required for public speaking. Next stop TV presenter? A single white cross stitch in each black eye patch creates just the right look.

nine Turn Preston over and position his tail at the back of his body so that the turning slit is facing the back of the body. Ladder stitch the bottom 4cm (1½in) of Preston's tail to secure (see page 106).

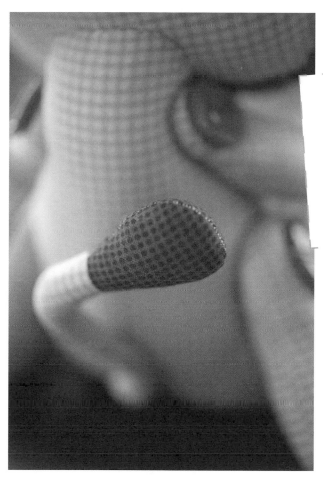

As Preston spends most of his time sitting down and pontificating, his tail is neatly parked in an upright position. For added visual interest, it has a contrasting-coloured tip, cleverly created by piecing together the two different fabrics before cutting out.

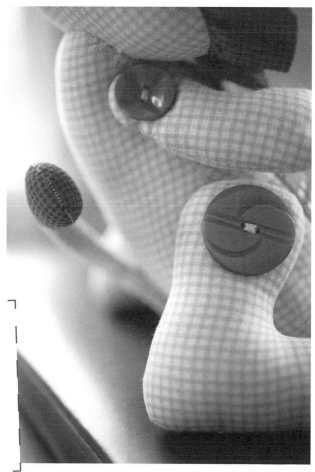

While Preston majors on matters of the head, he likes to use his arms and legs expressively to get his message across. This is why they are button jointed for flexibility – choose fancy coordinating buttons in keeping with his spruced-up image.

pearl the zebra

If there's a camera about, Pearl the Zebra will be there in a dash, posing for a shot or two in her latest outfit. Well, you've got to admit that she's got the body for it – those bold stripes are impressive. And it's hard not to notice that she's also something of a fashionista with her statement red pinafore and contrasting stylishly accessorized blouse.

There's lots to get stuck into here besides creating Pearl using the usual soft-toy making techniques – like making all her lovely clothes, which involves among other things lining the pinafore and making the bottom frill.

you will need

- 35cm (14in) x the full width of black and white striped cotton fabric (body, arms and legs)
- 5cm x 10cm (2in x 4in) each of black and white wool felt (eyes)
- 20cm x 71cm (8in x 28in) black and white checked cotton fabric (blouse)
- 30cm x 61cm (12in x 24in) black/floral cotton fabric (pantaloons)
- 30cm (12in) x the full width of red cotton fabric (pinafore)
- Small piece of fusible webbing
- Six-strand embroidery thread (floss): white, black
- 1 red button, 2.5cm (1in) diameter, optional
- Basic tool kit (see pages 102–103)

Finished size: about 50cm (20in) tall

'This is my best side'

one Trace all the templates for Pearl, including the outer eye and pupil, on pages 122–123 onto template plastic, transferring all the markings, and cut them out around the outside lines.

two Fold the black and white striped fabric in half horizontally, ensuring that the stripes meet accurately. Press. Draw around the body template once, then the arm, leg and ear templates twice each onto the folded fabric. **Don't cut out**, as these will be sewn before cutting out.

three Iron the fusible webbing to the wrong side of your black and white felt pieces. Draw around the outer eye and pupil templates twice each and cut out on the marked lines.

four Machine stitch the body together around the marked line, leaving the bottom open. Sew the arms and legs in the same way, leaving the ends open for turning. Sew the ears along the marked line, leaving the turning gap as indicated on the template.

five Cut out all the shapes approximately 6mm (¼ in) outside the stitched lines and snip the curved edges. Turn all the shapes right sides out.

six Stuff the legs firmly with toy filling up to the fill line, as indicated on the template (see pages 110). Machine stitch across the fill line. Bring seams at the bottom of Pearl's body to centre front and back. Insert the legs into the body, following the Inserting Legs technique on page 113. Stuff the body firmly. Ladder stitch the opening between the legs closed (see page 112).

> Pearl is understandably proud of her fine profile, with her neatly gathered ears and twinkling eyes – created with a carefully placed cross stitch.

seven Stuff the arms firmly to the fill line, as indicated on the template, then machine stitch across the fill line. Turn the ends of the arms in and stitch closed. Overstitch the arms to the side of the body, as indicated on the template.

eight Turn the raw ends of the ears in. Hand sew medium running stitches along the bottom edge, through both layers, without securing the thread end (see page 106). Pull the unsecured thread to gather the fabric evenly, then ladder stitch the ears in place, as indicated on the body template (see page 115).

nine Attach the eyes to Pearl's head as indicated on the body template by peeling off the backing paper and ironing on. Using three strands of white embroidery thread (floss), blanket stitch the outer eyes around the edges (see page 107). Repeat for the pupils with black thread (floss). Using white thread (floss), sew a cross stitch in each pupil (see page 107).

PEARL'S BLOUSE

one Fold the blouse fabric in half, right sides together. Draw around the blouse template once onto the folded fabric and cut out on the drawn line.

two Machine stitch the blouse pieces together, taking a 6mm (¼in) seam, from the top sleeve end to the neck markings on both sides, as indicated on the template. Then sew together from the bottom sleeve end up the arm and down the side seam on both sides. Clip under the arm and turn right side out. Press.

three Turn the neck opening under 6mm (¼in) and press. Using six strands of black or white embroidery thread (floss), hand sew medium running stitches around the sleeve ends, without securing the thread end. Place the blouse on Pearl, pull up the unsecured thread end to gather the sleeve fabric evenly and tie a knot to secure.

Tip

Sew a few small overstitches at each side of the blouse neckline to secure the turned-in neck opening if necessary.

four Using six strands of white embroidery thread (floss), sew a red button to the front of the blouse, taking the thread through the blouse into the body, then back through the blouse and the button. Tie in a reef (square) knot to secure (see page 109).

Pearl's choice of black and white checked blouse reveals her sound judgement about clothes, as it works well with her stripes and effectively contrasts with the red pinafore. And there's attention to detail too, in the gathered puff sleeves and the stylish button brooch.

PEARL'S PANTALOONS

ONE Fold the fabric for the pantaloons in half. Draw around the pantaloons template once onto the folded fabric and cut out on the marked line.

two Place the pantaloon pieces on top of each other, right sides together, and machine stitch together along both crotch seam lines, taking a 6mm (¼in) seam. Bring the front and back seams together and sew together from the bottom of one leg up to the crotch and back down the other leg. Turn right side out and press.

three Turn the waistband and leg bottoms under 1.25cm (½in). Hand sew medium running stitches around both, without securing the thread ends. Place the pantaloons on Pearl, pull up the unsecured thread ends to gather the fabric evenly and tie in a knot to secure – take a stitch into the body to ensure that the pantaloons won't fall down.

Now Pearl's showing off her pantaloons! Well, they certainly do make a splash with their flowery print on a black background, which keeps them working well with her body fabric.

PEARL'S PINAFORE

one Fold the pinafore fabric in half and draw around the pinafore template twice onto the folded fabric. Machine stitch two of the pinafore pieces right sides together around the central part of the neckline and the armholes, as shown in the diagram below. Repeat with the remaining two pinafore pieces. Snip the curved edges on both armholes and the sewn section of the neckline. Press.

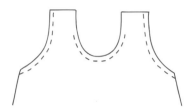

two Open up both the front and back of the pinafore and place on top of each other, right sides together. Sew together from the bottom of the main dress, up to the underarm and back down to the bottom of the lining on both sides of the pinafore, as indicated in the diagram below. Turn the pinafore right side out and push the lining inside the main dress.

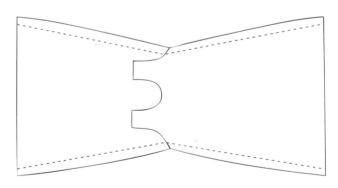

three Sew the shoulders of the pinafore front to the shoulders of the pinafore back by opening up the unstitched neckline on each section and meeting the raw edges of the shoulder seams. Press. Turn the raw edges of the neckline in and press. Topstitch the neckline, which will close the remaining gaps.

four Cut a strip of red fabric measuring 4cm (1½in) x the full width of the fabric. Remove the selvedges and fold the strip in half (end to end). Sew the ends together, creating a ring. Fold the ring in half, right sides out, all the way around and press.

five Set your sewing machine to the longest stitch and sew all around the double raw edge of the ring, without securing the thread end. Pull up the unsecured end to gather the fabric evenly so that it matches the bottom of the pinafore skirt.

six Open the pinafore out again and machine stitch the gathered ruffle to the main pinafore only. Press the ruffle down. Press the lining of the pinafore in by 6mm (¼in) and hand stitch or machine stitch the bottom of the lining to the bottom of the main pinafore. Place the pinafore on Pearl.

Tip

Make sure that the raw edges of the ruffle meet the raw edges at the bottom of the pinafore before you sew.

Pearl's desperate to perform a twirl in her designer dress for the camera, showing how it's beautifully lined and the bottom edge trimmed with a machine-gathered ruffle.

PEARL'S MANE

To create Pearl's mane, thread a double length of the full six strands of white embroidery thread (floss) through a large-eyed needle. Take a small stitch either side of the seam line at the top of Pearl's head. Tie the thread in a tight reef (square) knot (see page 109) and trim the ends to approximately 4cm (1½in) in length. Repeat along the seam line, as indicated on the body template.

She's a stunner all round, Pearl – even her mane is stylistic! But it's easy to create the desired effect using double lengths – that's 12 strands in total – of embroidery thread (floss), knotted and then trimmed.

darcy the dinosaur

You can't miss Darcy the Dinosaur – he's a larger-than-life character and no mistake. There he is, parading around displaying his fantastically patterned and coloured coat, not to mention his magnificent horn trio and the imposing frill around his neck. Darcy really is a grand animal – and he knows it!

You'll have great fun sourcing a suitably eye-popping printed fabric for Darcy's body – the bolder and quirkier the better. But then he's straightforward to construct, being an all-in-one toy, although his legs will need extra-firm stuffing to ensure that they are sturdy enough to keep him strutting his stuff.

you will need

- 25cm (10in) x the full width of blue patterned fabric (head, body)

- 13cm x 25cm (5in x 10in) red patterned fabric (frill)

- Small scrap of plain white homespun fabric (horns)

- 13cm x 13cm (5in x 5in) lightweight fusible fleece interlining

- 25cm (10in) large blue ric-rac

- Black six-strand embroidery thread (floss)

- Basic tool kit (see pages 102–103)

Finished size: about 40cm (16in) long x 20cm (8in) tall

It's easy to see why Darcy the dandy just loves to impress onlookers with his neck frill. The large ric-rac used for the edging is a quick and easy way to achieve an evenly shaped outline.

one Trace all the templates for Darcy from page 117 onto template plastic, transferring any markings, and cut them out around the outside lines.

two Fold the blue patterned fabric in half, right sides together. Draw around the body, head and inner leg templates once each onto the folded fabric. Cut out the shapes along the marked lines. Transfer the dart markings to the wrong side of the inner leg pieces.

three Fold the red fabric in half, right sides together. Draw around the frill template once onto the folded fabric. Iron the fusible fleece interlining to the back half of the folded fabric. Cut out the frill pieces around the marked line. Take both of the frill pieces and place them on top of

each other, right sides together. Place the length of ric-rac between the two layers, starting and ending at the star, as indicated on the template, centring the ric-rac in the frill to give an even finish. Pin in place. Sew the frill together, capturing the ric-rac and leaving the inner curve open, as indicated on the template. Turn right side out and press.

four Take one body piece and one inner leg piece and place on top of each other, right sides together. You will notice that the top of the inner leg pieces are slightly narrower than the body pieces, so you will need to tack (baste) the edges in place so that the raw edges meet. Machine stitch together, starting to sew right at the raw edge of the fabric, gradually taking a 6mm (¼in) seam and then tapering to the raw edge again at the other end, as shown below.

Tip

If you like, you can topstitch some lines around the frill, from the inner curve out to meet the ric-rac curves.

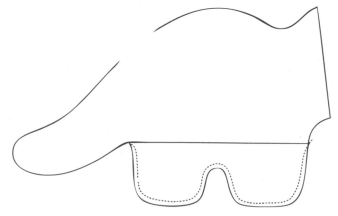

five Repeat Step 4 with the remaining body and inner leg pieces. Snip the curve in the inner legs. **Don't turn right sides out.**

six Fold one of the inner leg sections in half, right sides together, so that the fold falls down the centre of one of the dart markings. Machine stitch the dart in place following your markings. Repeat with the remaining three inner leg darts. Trim any excess fabric away from the darts.

seven Place the two body pieces on top of each other, right sides together, with the inner legs in between. Machine stitch the top edge of Darcy's body together from the turning gap, as marked on the template, to the top neckline only, taking a 6mm (¼in) seam.

eight Place the two head pieces on top of each other, right sides together. Machine stitch together from the top neckline to the marked star only.

He may be the best-dressed beast on the planet, but Darcy's no lounge lizard, as you can see here. Stuffed with the right density of top-quality filling, he's as sturdy as soft toys come.

nine Place the necklines of the body and head on top of each other, right sides together, ensuring that the seams meet. Place the frill between the two layers so that the inner raw edge of the frill meets the raw edges of the neckline. Start tacking (basting) the layers together at the centre of the frill, which will meet the sewn seam lines. Working from the centre out, ease the necklines into the curve of the frill, tacking (basting) as you go. Machine stitch the complete neckline together, capturing the frill in your sewing.

ten Reposition the two body/head pieces so that they are evenly on top of each other, right sides together, with the inner legs in between. Tack (baste) together, from the back end of the turning gap to the marked star on the nose (the end of the previous sewing). When you reach the inner leg section, make sure that you are tacking (basting) the top edges of the inner legs together, right sides facing – it may be easier to fold the legs up against either side of the body (see the diagram below).

No wonder Darcy's so vain – he looks so cool from every conceivable angle. His neck frill is sewn into the body/head neckline for a neat and secure finish.

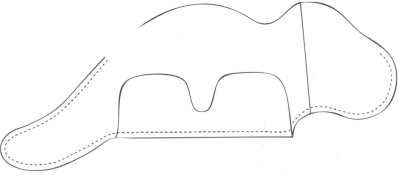

eleven Sew the body together, leaving the turning gap open. Turn right side out. Stuff very firmly with filling (see pages 110), then ladder stitch the opening closed (see page 112), filling a bit more as you go to avoid a dimple.

Darcy considers his horns his next best feature after his neck frill, but there's really no end to his vanity. Being quite narrow, turning the fabric pieces is a little tricky, but you'll find the technique on page 111 a big help.

twelve Fold the white fabric in half, right sides together. Draw around the smaller horn template, for Darcy's nose, once and the larger horn, for Darcy's head, twice onto the folded fabric. Machine stitch the horns together along the drawn lines, leaving the ends open for turning. Cut the horn shapes out approximately 3mm (⅛in) outside your drawn lines and turn right side out, following the Turning Small Pieces technique on page 111.

thirteen Turn the raw ends of the horns in by approximately 6mm (¼in) and then stuff the horns firmly with toy filling. Following the Attaching Parts with Ladder Stitch technique on page 115, ladder stitch the folded edge of the horns onto Darcy's head and nose.

fourteen Mark the eye circles on Darcy's face with a vanishing marker or grey lead pencil, as marked on the template, and then satin stitch the circles using two strands of black embroidery thread (floss) (see page 107).

Look, Darcy's trying to catch your eye so that you can admire him all the more. Being worked in satin stitch using only black embroidery (thread) gives his eyes an alluring depth.

mabelle the mouse

A far cry from the traditional timid image, Mabelle is a mouse with a big personality – that's easy to tell from the size of her fabulous pink and yellow ears and her flamboyantly patterned body with contrasting tummy spot. Watch out, this radical rodent is up for all kinds of fun and games!

Mabelle's arms and feet are stuffed and tacked (basted) in position on the body front before her body and head are sewn together. A circle of thick cardboard inserted into the base of Mabelle's body allows her to stand firmly on a flat surface, underlining her bold, robust nature.

you will need

- 20cm (8in) x the full width of blue floral patterned fabric (main body)
- 13cm x 13cm (5in x 5in) yellow patterned fabric (tummy spot, inner ears)
- 13cm (5in) x the full width of pink patterned fabric (feet, arms, ears, nose)
- 13cm x 13cm (5in x 5in) fusible webbing
- 13cm x 25.5cm (5in x 10in) lightweight fusible fleece interlining
- 10cm x 10cm (4in x 4in) thick cardboard
- Six-strand embroidery thread (floss): black, blue
- 18cm (7in) cotton cord in a matching colour (tail)
- Basic tool kit (see pages 102–103)

Finished size: 21cm (8¼in) tall

'Now you see me...'

three Take one of your head front pieces and sew the dart together on the wrong side of the fabric as marked, then press. Repeat with the remaining head front piece and two head back pieces.

four Place the head front pieces on top of each other, right sides together, so that the raw edges and darts meet. Machine stitch together along the centre head seam, taking a 6mm (¼in) seam. Repeat with the head back pieces.

five Place two of the body pieces on top of each other, right sides together. Tie a knot in one end of the cotton cord. Lay between the two body pieces so that it is approximately 2.5cm (1in) up from the bottom edge and the unknotted end meets the raw edges on the centre body edge. Sew together along the centre body seam, capturing the cord in the process, to create a tail. Repeat with the remaining two body pieces (without the cord) for the body front.

one Trace all the templates for Mabelle from page 119 onto template plastic, transferring all the markings, and cut them all out around the outside lines.

two Fold the blue floral patterned fabric in half, right sides together. Draw around the body template twice, the head front template once and the head back template once onto the folded fabric and cut out. Unfold the remaining fabric, draw around the base template onto the single fabric and cut out.

six Cut a piece of yellow patterned fabric measuring 7.5cm x 7.5cm (3in x 3in) and iron fusible webbing to the wrong side. Draw around the tummy spot template onto the paper side and cut out. Centre the tummy spot on the body front, peel away the paper and iron into place. Machine appliqué the tummy spot to secure in position (see page 108).

Mabelle is justifiably proud of her lovely long tail, so she won't like you tugging at it! However, should you be tempted, it's very securely, and neatly, joined to her body by being sewn into the centre body seam. Choose cotton cord in a shade that tones with the main body fabric.

SEVEN Fold the pink patterned fabric in half, right sides together. Draw around the foot and arm template twice each onto the wrong side. Machine stitch along the marked lines, leaving the ends open for turning as indicated. Cut the shapes out approximately 6mm (¼in) outside the sewn lines. Turn right side out. Stuff the arms and feet firmly with toy filling (see pages 110), leaving the open ends lightly filled. Tack (baste) the stuffing holes closed.

'...now you don't!'

eight Place one arm, right side up, over the left-hand side of the body front, also right side up, so that the hand faces in towards the tummy. The top raw edge of the arm should rest on the top raw edge of the body and begin approximately 1.25 (½in) in from the left-hand side edge of the body front. Tack (baste) into place. Repeat for the right arm (see the diagram on the right).

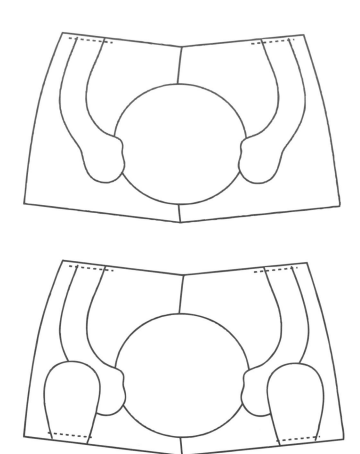

nine Place one foot over the left-hand side of the body front, right sides together, so that the foot faces in towards the tummy. The raw edge of the foot should meet the bottom raw edge of the body and begin approximately 2.5cm (1in) in from the left-hand side edge of the body front. Tack (baste) into place. Repeat for the right foot (see the diagram on the right).

ten Place the body back and head back on top of each other, right sides together, so that the neck edges meet. Machine stitch together along the neck seam. Repeat for the body front and head front, ensuring that the arms are captured in the seam.

eleven Place Mabelle's front and back on top of each other, right sides together. Machine stitch together from the bottom of the body, up and over the top of the head and back down to the bottom of the body, leaving the bottom edge open for the base. **Don't turn right side out.**

twelve Take the body base and ease into position, right sides together, evenly along the bottom edge of Mabelle's body. Tack (baste) and then sew the base into position from one edge of the turning gap, as marked on the template, to the other. Turn Mabelle right side out through the gap in the base.

thirteen Trace the inner base template onto thick cardboard and cut out. Insert the inner base into Mabelle through the turning gap and lay against the base.

Has Mabelle been over-adventurous and taken a tumble? Why no – you can see how sturdy she is underneath. She's just rolling around on her back, having fun while the cat's away!

fourteen Keeping the base in position as you go, stuff Mabelle firmly with toy filling. Ladder stitch the turning gap closed (see page 112).

fifteen Iron fusible webbing to the wrong side of the remaining yellow patterned fabric. Draw around the inner ear template twice on the paper side and cut out. Fold the remaining pink patterned fabric in half, right sides together. Draw around the main ear template twice onto the fabric and cut out. Take one of the pink ear pieces, peel away the paper backing from one of the yellow inner ears and iron in place on the right side. Machine appliqué to secure in position. Repeat for the second ear.

sixteen Draw around the main ear template twice onto fusible fleece interlining and cut out. Iron onto the wrong side of the remaining two pink ear pieces.

You can see just how mischievous Mabelle is from her cheeky-looking expression, and her crazy oversize ears give her an endearing comical air. These are reinforced with iron-on fleece interlining to ensure that they remain 'outstanding'!

seventeen Place one of the main ear with inner ear pieces and one with interlining on top of each other, right sides together. Sew the ear together, leaving the turning gap open as indicated on the template. Snip the corners, turn right side out and press. Repeat for the second ear.

eighteen Hand sew medium running stitches along the bottom edge of one ear, without securing the thread at the end (see page 106). Pull the unsecured end to gather up the fabric evenly, then ladder stitch the ear into position on the side of Mabelle's head (see page 115). Repeat with the second ear.

Tip

It's a good idea to ladder stitch each ear from the front and again from the back for added strength.

MABELLE'S FEATURES

one Mark Mabelle's eyes onto her face with a pencil and then satin stitch using two strands of black embroidery thread (floss) (see page 107).

two For Mabelle's snout, from the remaining pink patterned fabric, cut a circle measuring about 5cm (2in) in diameter. Hand stitch all the way around the circle, approximately 6mm (¼in) in from the raw edge, and pull to gather up the fabric, as in Step 18 opposite, then lightly stuff. Fold in the raw edges and fit the snout over Mabelle's nose. Stuffing and gathering a little more as you go, ladder stitch the snout onto Mabelle's face (see page 106).

three For Mabelle's whiskers, tie a knot in three strands of blue embroidery thread (floss) approximately 2.5cm (1in) from the end. Pass the needle through Mabelle's face from one side to the other, just behind her pink snout, until the knot stops it. Tie another knot where the thread exits the other side of the face and then trim to 2.5cm (1in) outside the knot. Repeat twice more.

Tip

If using a large floral fabric for the main body, choose a tiny print in a high-contrast colour for the remaining parts to achieve maximum definition.

This is clearly a snout for sniffing out the main action, with whiskers to give extra guidance. Mabelle's snout is simply a lightly stuffed gathered circle of fabric, and the whiskers are strands of embroidery thread (floss).

gerbera the giraffe

Cats are well known for their curiosity, but giraffes?
This pretty, prancing giraffe called Gerbera certainly has an inquisitive side to her nature, although she can be a bit jumpy and bound off if things go horribly wrong as a consequence of her investigations.

As well as the usual basic sewing techniques, simple gathering is used to good effect here in creating Gerbera's frilly mane and attractively shaped ears. She may be spotted like her wild cousins, but her cover is easily blown with her coat of a heady mix of bright colours and patterns.

you will need

- 15cm (6in) x the full width of white spotted fabric (hooves, ears, mane, tail)
- 40cm (16in) x the full width of blue patterned fabric (main body)
- 13cm x 13cm (5in x 5in) plain red cotton fabric (horns)
- Six-strand embroidery thread (floss): black, blue
- 2 black buttons, 1.25cm (½in) diameter (don't use if making for a small child)
- Basic tool kit (see pages 102–103)

Finished size: 40cm (16in) tall

one Trace all the templates for Gerbera from the page 116 onto template plastic, transferring all the markings, and cut them out around the outside lines.

two From the white spotted fabric, cut one strip measuring 6.5cm (2½in) x the width of the fabric. With right sides together, machine stitch the strip along the bottom of the entire 40cm (16in) of blue patterned fabric and press. Fold the fabric panel in half, right sides together, so that the fabrics and seams meet.

three Draw around the main body template and inner leg template once onto the wrong side of your folded fabric panel, lining up the bottom of the templates with the bottom raw edge of the white spotted fabric. Cut out on the outside line to give you two main body pieces and two inner leg pieces.

four Place one main body piece and one inner leg piece on top of each other, right sides together. You will notice that the top of the inner leg pieces are slightly narrower than the body pieces, so you will need to tack (baste) the edges in place so that the raw edges meet.

Tip

To avoid any puckering, rotate and smooth Gerbera's leg constantly as you sew the hoof base to the leg.

five Machine stitch the inner leg to the main body, starting right at the raw edge of the fabric and gradually forming a 6mm (¼in) seam, then tapering the stitching line to the raw edge again at the other end, as shown in the diagram below. Don't sew the bottom edges of the hooves together. Trim the corners and snip the curves. Repeat with the remaining body and inner leg pieces, **but don't turn either right side out.**

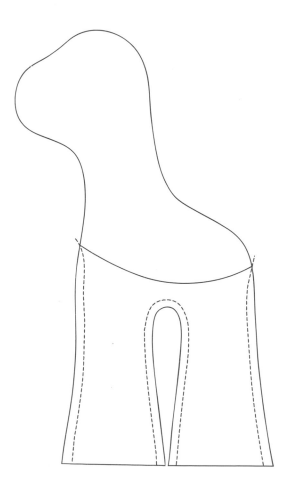

six Draw around the hoof base template four times onto the remaining white spotted fabric and cut out. Take one of the hoof bases and ease this into place, right sides together, along the base on one of Gerbera's legs. When you are happy with the fit, tack (baste) or thoroughly pin in place before machine stitching.

seven For the mane, cut a strip of white spotted fabric measuring 4cm x 50cm (1½in x 20in). Fold the strip in half, right side out, all the way along the length and press. Hand sew medium running stitches along the raw edges of the folded strip, without securing the thread at the end (see page 106). Pull the unsecured end to gather up the fabric strip evenly until it measures approximately 25.5cm (10in) in length and then machine stitch the raw edge to secure the ruffles in place.

Although she might sometimes take a step too far, Gerbera's such a colourful character, she's even got brightly coloured spotted hooves! Choose a printed fabric that gives a good contrast with the main body fabric but nevertheless has a colour link, as here.

Just like a real giraffe's, Gerbera's mane is short and neat, easily made from a gathered-up strip of the same spotted fabric used for her hooves.

eight Take one of the main body pieces and place the mane, right sides together, along Gerbera's neck. The raw edge of the mane should lay against the raw edge of the neck and the mane should taper away from the head and neck at the start and end, as shown in the diagram on the right. Machine stitch the mane in place. Trim the ends.

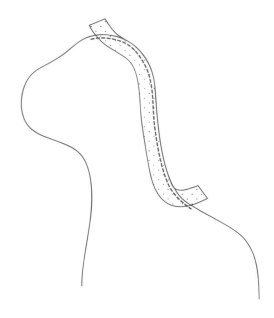

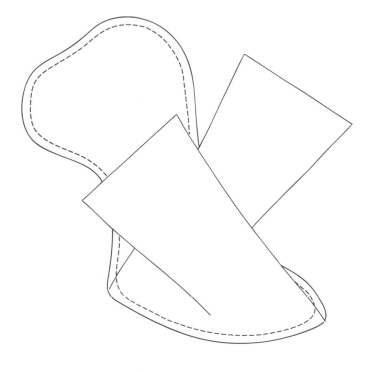

nine Place the two body pieces on top of each other, right sides together, with the inner legs in between. Tack (baste) the body pieces together, starting from one end of the turning gap to the other. When you reach the inner leg section, you need to ensure that you are tacking (basting) the top straight edges of the inner legs together, right sides facing (see the diagram on the left).

ten Sew the body together, leaving the turning gap open. Snip the curved and angled edges and then turn right side out.

eleven Stuff the body firmly with toy filling (see page 110) and then ladder stitch the opening closed, filling a little more as you go (see page 112).

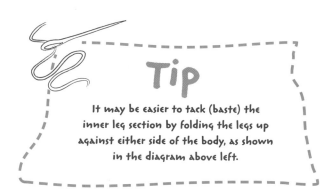

Tip

It may be easier to tack (baste) the inner leg section by folding the legs up against either side of the body, as shown in the diagram above left.

'I wish I was just a bit taller!'

twelve Draw around the horn template twice onto the wrong side of the plain red fabric folded in half. Sew the horns together along the marked line, leaving the ends open for turning as indicated on the template. Cut the horns out approximately 3mm (⅛in) outside the sewn lines. Turn the horns right side out and stuff firmly with toy filling.

thirteen Fold the bottom raw edges inside the horns and then, following the Attaching Parts with Ladder Stitch technique on page 115, ladder stitch the folded edges onto Gerbera's head. Sew one horn approximately 6mm (¼in) to the left of the beginning of the mane and the other the same distance to the right side of the mane, making sure that you stitch them in a circle to retain the rounded horn shape.

fourteen Take a small piece of the remaining white spotted fabric and fold in half, right sides together. Draw around the ear template twice onto the wrong side and sew the ears together along the marked lines, leaving the bottom edge open as indicated on the template. Cut the ears out approximately 6mm (¼in) outside the sewn lines. Snip the corners, turn right side out and press.

Our lively giraffe friend is always on the alert for adventure, ears and eyes primed, ready to spring into action. Gerbera's gathered ears are in the contrasting spotted fabric, while the stuffed horns stand out well in a plain red fabric. The button eyes can be replaced with satin-stitched (see page 108) or black wool felt ones for a small child.

Tip

Pull the thread tight when sewing on the button eyes if you want them to dimple the head a little.

fifteen Hand stitch and pull the thread end to gather the bottom edges of the ears, as in Step 7 on page 71. Ladder stitch one ear onto either side of Gerbera's head, each ear beginning about 6mm (¼in) from a horn.

sixteen Using all six strands of a length of black embroidery thread (floss), attach a black button to either side of the head as an eye. This can be done using the same method as button jointing, sewing through the head (see page 114).

Gerbera is flicking her tail enthusiastically in anticipation of uncovering something interesting in her explorations. Lengths of blue embroidery thread (floss) make a nicely tactile tuft emerging from the end of the stubby stuffed part of the tail.

seventeen To make the tail, cut two small pieces of white spotted fabric measuring 4.5cm x 2.5cm (1¾in x 1in). Take about ten 8–10cm (3–4in) lengths of blue embroidery thread (floss) and place between the two fabric pieces, right sides together. Sew the tail together along both long and one short end, capturing the thread (floss) in the short end stitches, as shown in the diagram above. Turn right side out, stuff the tail and trim the threads to the desired length. Fold the bottom raw edges inside the tail and then ladder stitch the tail onto Gerbera's rear.

alvin the alien

Look who's just landed from a far-off planet. It's Alvin the Alien – a much more colourful character than your average little green man, and as friendly and cuddly as extra-terrestrials come. Despite his weird head with one too many eyes than normal, he's eager to waddle over on his flipper-like feet and embrace you with his three-digit hands.

Alvin is easy to make, his body cut from a panel of fabric that incorporates stitched-together strips of contrastingly patterned fabrics for his eye-catching torso. Simple wool felt shapes are used for his bulging eyes and basic embroidery stitches for his cute nose, jagged mouth and lolling tongue.

you will need

- 20cm (8in) x the full width of green patterned fabric (body, arms)
- 3 strips of contrasting patterned fabric, 4cm x 50cm (1½in x 20in) each (body)
- Small scraps of wool felt: white, black (eyes)
- 13cm x 13cm (5in x 5in) fusible webbing
- Six-strand embroidery thread (floss): red, black, white
- Basic tool kit (see pages 102–103)

Finished size: 28cm (11in) tall

one Trace the main Alvin template and the arm template from page 116 onto template plastic, transferring all the markings, and cut out around the outside lines. Cut out separate templates for the upper outer eye and pupil and the middle outer eye and pupil.

Tip

Make sure that each strip of patterned fabric accurately measures 4cm x 50cm (1½in x 20in).

two From the green patterned fabric, cut one panel measuring 18cm x 50cm (7in x 20in) and one measuring 10cm x 50cm (4in x 20in).

three Using a 6mm (¼in) seam and a very small stitch, machine stitch the three strips of contrasting patterned fabric together along the long edges, and to the two pieces of green patterned fabric, as shown in the diagram on the right, to create a pieced panel. Press.

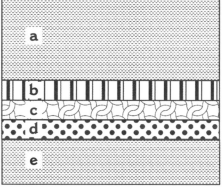

a) Green patterned fabric
18cm x 50cm (7in x 20in)

b) Contrasting patterned fabric
4cm x 50cm (1½in x 20in)

c) Contrasting patterned fabric
4cm x 50cm (1½in x 20in)

d) Contrasting patterned fabric
4cm x 50cm (1½in x 20in)

e) Green patterned fabric
10cm x 50cm (4in x 20in)

Tip

This is a great opportunity to use up any scraps of printed fabrics you might have put by. Choose three very different, bold patterns to make your version of Alvin suitably eye-boggling, but ensure that they are complementary in terms of colour.

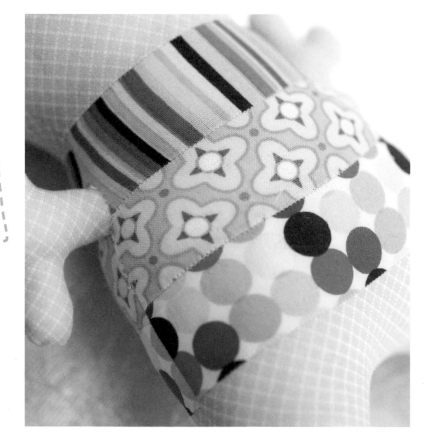

four Fold your pieced panel in half, right sides together, ensuring that all the seams meet accurately, and press in place. Mark the outside line of the main Alvin template on the wrong side of the folded fabric panel, ensuring that your seam lines match up with the lines on the template.

five Open the fabric panel out and place it, right side up, onto a light box or other light source, such as a window. Place the main Alvin template under the fabric and match up the marked outside line with the template outside line.

On the right-hand side of your fabric, carefully mark the mouth, tongue, nose and three outer eyes.

six Using two strands of red embroidery thread (floss), satin stitch the tongue in place (see page 107). Using all six strands of black embroidery thread (floss), backstitch the mouth and nose (see page 106). Using two strands of black embroidery thread (floss), outline the tongue and stitch the central tongue line over the satin stitching in backstitch.

It looks like Alvin's a little hungry, judging by his satin-stitched tongue hanging out. Just hope he isn't thinking of you as lunch – that craggy mouth of his is, after all, noticeably large...

seven Take the piece of white wool felt and iron fusible webbing to the wrong side of it. Draw around the upper outer eye template twice and the middle outer eye template once onto the paper side and cut out.

eight Take the piece of black wool felt and iron fusible webbing to the wrong side of it. Trace the upper eye pupil template twice and the middle eye pupil template once onto the paper side and cut out.

nine Peel the paper from the back of all your wool felt pieces and position the eyes on Alvin's face, ensuring that you place them exactly as previously marked. Press into place with your iron. Secure the outer eyes and pupils around the outside edges with blanket stitch on your sewing machine using matching thread, or blanket stitch by hand using two strands of matching embroidery thread (floss) (see page 107).

ten Using six strands of white embroidery thread (floss), add a double-wrap French knot to each eye as indicated on the template (see page 107).

eleven Fold your main body panel in half again, right sides together, and pin to ensure that all the seams remain together. Sew the body together along the marked outside line by stitching with a small stitch on your sewing machine, leaving the turning gap open as indicated on the template.

twelve Cut the body shape out from your fabric panel, approximately 6mm (¼in) outside the sewn line. Snip all the curved and angled edges.

thirteen Turn the body right side out and then stuff firmly with toy filling (see page 110). Ladder stitch the opening closed (see page 112), filling a little more as you go.

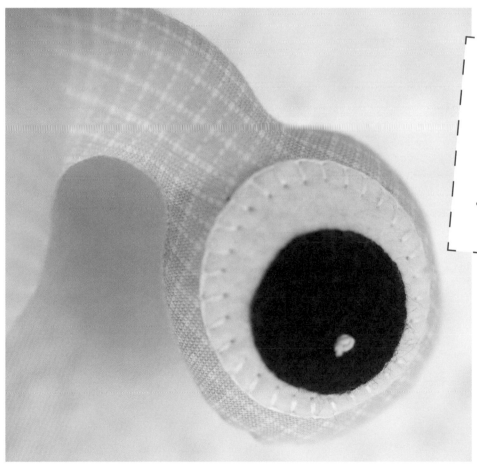

Alvin can ogle you from three different directions at once! And there's a real twinkle in his eye(s), an impression convincingly achieved by the clever positioning of an embroidered double-wrap French knot.

fourteen Fold the remaining green fabric in half and draw around the arm template twice onto the wrong side of the fabric, **but don't cut out.**

fifteen Sew Alvin's arms together by machine stitching along the marked lines with a very small stitch, leaving the turning gaps at the end open as indicated on the template. Cut out approximately 3–6mm (⅛–¼in) outside the stitched line and then snip the curved and angled edges. Turn right side out.

sixteen Stuff the arms firmly with toy filling. Turn the raw edges of the arms in. Following the Attaching Parts with Ladder Stitch technique on page 115, ladder stitch the arms to the sides of Alvin's body in a circle, referring to the photo below right for their positioning.

Tip

Go over your stitching of the arms to the body twice, for added strength.

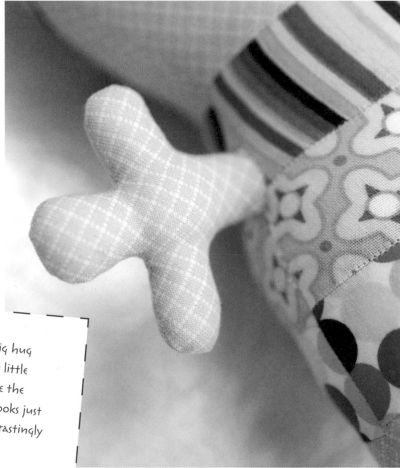

Watch out, Alvin's coming to give you a big hug – well, as big as it can be with those stubby little arms. These need to be firmly stuffed to give the right outstretched effect (see page 110). He looks just as jolly from behind, with the panel of contrastingly patterned strips extending round his back.

polly the pig

Watch out, Polly the Pig's about, and she's a powerhouse of energy, so you're in serious danger of being bowled over by her. Don't let her rather stout physique fool you – she's a real whiz kid, bustling around the place and eager to get involved in anything that's going down. In fact, she's a bit of a speed junkie. You've been warned – keep those skateboards securely under wraps!

Polly is another easy all-in-one design, with even her ears and tail being sewn into her main body pieces in one go. Only her lightly stuffed nose is sewn on as a separate entity at the end.

you will need

- 20cm (8in) x the full width of pink patterned fabric (main body)
- 13cm x 30cm (5in x 12in) light striped fabric (nose, ear, tail)
- Small scrap of pink wool felt
- Small scrap of fusible webbing
- Pink six-strand embroidery thread (floss), optional
- 1 pipe cleaner
- 2 black buttons, 1.25cm (½in) diameter, optional
- Basic tool kit (see pages 102–103)

Finished size: about 15cm (6in) tall

'Can this go any faster?'

oNe Trace all the templates for Polly from page 119 onto template plastic, transferring any markings, and cut them out around the outside lines.

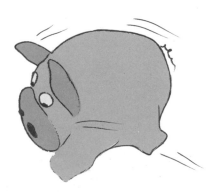

Such a dynamic character as Polly needs a high-impact fabric combo to match, and the uniformly striped print of her ears and snout makes a really effective contrast against the randomly splodgy, busy pattern of her body.

two Fold the pink patterned fabric in half, right sides together. Draw around the main body and inner leg templates once onto the folded fabric. Cut out the shapes along the drawn lines. Transfer the dart markings to the wrong side of the inner leg pieces.

three Fold the light striped fabric in half, right sides together. Draw around the ear template twice onto the folded fabric. Machine stitch the ears together by sewing along the marked lines, leaving the bottom straight edge open for turning. Cut the ears out approximately 6mm (¼in) outside the sewn lines. Snip the point, turn right side out and press.

four Take one of the ears and fold the bottom corners in to meet at the centre bottom edge. You can also create a small pleat in the centre of the ear. Tack (baste) the folds and the pleat in place. Repeat with the remaining ear, making sure that your pleat is the mirror image of the first ear.

Polly's ears are neatly folded and pleated – a bit like a paper dart, so perhaps they are aerodynamic enough to give her extra speed!

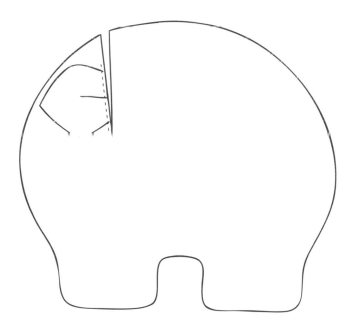

five Take one of the main body pieces and place one of Polly's ears, right sides together, onto the front of the head dart edge, as shown in the diagram above. The raw edge of the ear should meet the raw edge of the dart and be approximately 2.5cm (1in) down from the top of Polly's head. Tack (baste) the ear in place.

six Fold this main body piece, right sides together, so that the raw edges of the head dart meet evenly. Sew the dart in place, capturing the ear in the seam in the process. Repeat the procedure with the remaining ear and main body piece.

seven For Polly's tail, cut a small strip of your light striped fabric measuring approximately 4cm x 9cm (1½in x 3½in). Fold in half, right sides together, along the length. Sew the strip together along one short and the long raw edge, leaving one short end open. Snip the corners and turn, following the Turning Small Pieces technique on page 111.

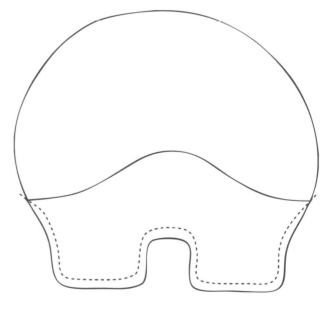

Polly's tail may not add to her speed, but it's suitably swiggly to match her lively personality. It's ingeniously made out of a twisted length of pipe cleaner inserted into a fabric tube.

eight Take a length of the pipe cleaner measuring approximately 18cm (7in). Fold the pipe cleaner onto itself and twist to wind it together. Insert the folded end of the pipe cleaner into the striped fabric tube. Cut away any excess pipe cleaner outside the tube. Position the tail on one of the main body pieces, right sides together, as indicated on the template. The raw end of the tail tube should meet the raw edge of Polly's rear. Tack (baste) the tail in place.

nine Place one main body piece and one inner leg piece on top of each other, right sides together. Sew the inner leg to the main body, starting to sew right at the raw edge of the fabric, gradually taking a 6mm (¼in) seam and then tapering to the raw edge again at the other end, as shown in the diagram above right. Repeat with the remaining body and inner leg piece. **Don't turn right sides out.**

ten Take one of the inner leg sections and fold in half, right sides together, so that the fold falls down the centre of the dart marking. Sew the dart in place in the inner leg only. Repeat with the remaining inner leg piece. Trim any excess fabric away from the darts.

eleven Place the two body pieces on top of each other, right sides together, with the inner legs in between. Tack (baste) the body pieces together, starting from one end of the marked turning gap to the other. When you reach the inner leg section, make sure that you are tacking (basting) the top edges of the inner legs together, right sides facing. It may be easier to do this by folding the legs up against either side of the body (see the diagram on the right). The tail should be lying between the two body layers.

twelve Machine stitch Polly's body together, leaving the turning gap open. Snip the curved and angled edges, then turn right side out. Stuff the body very firmly with toy filling (see page 110) and then ladder stitch the opening closed, filling a bit more as you go to avoid a dimple (see page 112).

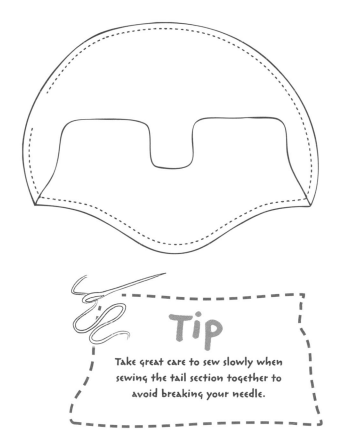

Tip

Take great care to sew slowly when sewing the tail section together to avoid breaking your needle.

Polly's 'go-faster' legs need some seriously firm stuffing to ensure that they are sturdy enough to keep her on the move.

thirteen Draw around the nose template twice onto the remaining light striped fabric. Cut out the shapes along the drawn lines.

fourteen Iron fusible webbing onto the wrong side of your scrap of pink wool felt. Draw around the nostril template twice onto the paper side of the fusible webbing and cut out along the drawn lines. Peel the backing paper away and position the nostril circles onto one of the nose pieces. Press the nostrils into place. Either machine blanket stitch (or zigzag stitch if your machine doesn't do blanket stitch) the nostrils into position around the edges with pink polyester thread or hand blanket stitch using two strands of pink embroidery thread (floss) (see page 107).

fifteen Place the two nose pieces on top of each other, right sides together. Machine stitch together all the way around the edge. Cut a slit 1.75cm (¾in) in length into the centre back of the nose only – don't cut the side with the nostrils! Turn the nose right side out using the slit.

Polly has an appropriately prominent snout, since she not only busies about but is a busybody, thriving on nosing around in other people's business! See here how it's neatly and securely stitched into place using ladder stitch and strong polyester thread.

sixteen Stuff the nose lightly through the slit in the back. Position the nose on Polly's face so that the turning gaps in both the head and nose are hidden. Pin the nose into position and then ladder stitch into place along the back nose edge, approximately 3mm (⅛in) from the sewn seam, following Attaching Parts with Ladder Stitch on page 115.

seventeen Sew the black buttons in place on Polly's face as eyes. However, if you are making this toy for a small child, omit the buttons and create the pupils with appliquéd circles of black wool felt (as for the nose in Step 14), or by embroidering in satin stitch or using a double-wrap French knot (see page 107).

'Let's go, go go!'

finnegan the frog

Come and meet this fab-looking fellow, Finnegan the Frog, who likes nothing else but to indulge in fun in the sun. You only have to look at that big smiley face and then at his playfully printed fabric body and boldly patterned surfer shorts to see that he means serious recreational business!

A range of straight-forward soft toy-making techniques are involved in creating Finnegan – all explained at the back of the book (see pages 106–115), including sewing several pattern pieces together, stuffing and attaching limbs, together with basic embroidery stitches to add his expressive facial features.

you will need

- 40cm (16in) x the full width of green patterned fabric (body, arms, legs)
- 18cm x 18cm (7in x 7in) green linen/cotton blend fabric (face)
- 25.5cm x 25.5cm (10in x 10in) red patterned fabric (shorts)
- 10cm x 10cm (4in x 4in) fusible webbing
- 10cm x 10cm (4in x 4in) white wool felt (eyes)
- Small scrap of black wool felt (eyes)
- Six-strand embroidery thread (floss): white, black
- 2 buttons in a matching colour, 2.5cm (1in) diameter (don't use if making for a small child)
- Fabric glue
- Basic tool kit (see pages 102–103)

Finished size: 42cm (16½in) tall

'Lovely day for a swim!'

one Trace all the templates for Finnegan from page 118 onto template plastic, transferring all the markings, and cut them out around the outside lines. Cut out separate templates for the eye and pupil.

two From the green patterned fabric, draw around the body and head top templates once onto the fabric folded in half, then draw around the face back once onto single fabric. Cut these pieces out.

three Draw around the leg and arm templates twice each onto the remaining green patterned fabric folded in half, **but don't cut out.**

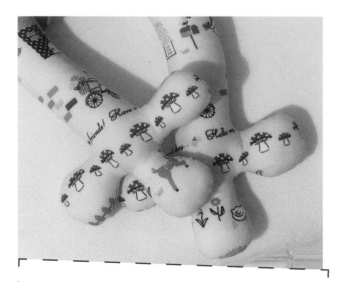

Finnegan's funky limbs, with their three round, fat toes/fingers, are not really built for agility or hard work, but they're just perfect for hanging out round the pool! Remember not to cut the fabric pieces out after you have drawn around the templates, as they are sewn together before cutting out.

Tip

For Finnegan's body fabric, you can use a really quirky print to great effect, as the one chosen here, to give your frog friend a really zany look. Even though lime green is in the finest frog tradition, it can be any colour you like.

four From the green linen/cotton blend fabric, draw around the face front template once onto the single fabric and transfer the dart markings.

five Take the face front and sew the darts together on the wrong side of your fabric as marked. Trim the excess fabric and press.

six Place the face front and one of the head top pieces on top of each other, right sides together. Ensuring that the head top is centrally placed, pin or tack (baste) it into place while easing the curve into the curve of the face as you go. Machine stitch together and press.

'This is the life!'

seven Place the completed head on top of the front body piece, right sides together. Ensuring that the body neckline is centrally placed, pin or tack (baste) it into place while easing the curve into the curve of the face as you go. Sew together and press. Repeat Step 6 on page 94 and this step with the face back, head top and body back pieces.

eight Place the completed frog front and back on top of each other, right sides together, ensuring that all the seams meet. Sew the body together along all the edges, leaving the bottom edge of the body open for turning. Snip any curved or angled edges. Turn right side out.

nine Sew the arms and legs together by sewing along the marked lines, leaving the turning gaps open as indicated. Cut out approximately 6mm (¼in) outside the stitched lines and snip the curved and angled edges. Turn right side out.

ten Stuff the arms firmly with toy filling (see page 110) and then ladder stitch the opening closed (see page 112). Stuff the legs firmly up to the fill line and then sew across the fill line with your sewing machine.

eleven Following the Inserting Legs technique on page 113, sew the legs into either side of the open bottom edge of the body. Stuff the head and body firmly with toy filling, using the opening between the legs as your stuffing hole. Ladder stitch the opening between the legs closed, stuffing a little more as you go if required.

twelve Following the Button Jointing technique on page 114, attach the arms to either side of the top of Finnegan's body, using suitably coloured buttons.

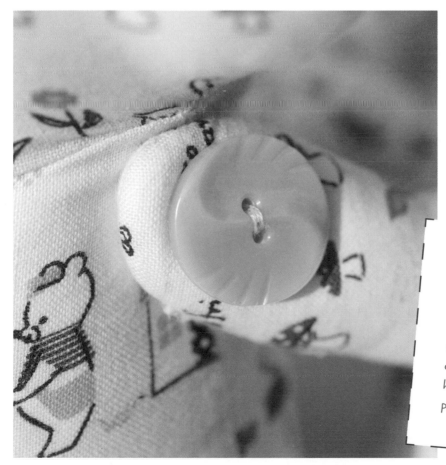

Button jointing is a simple, strong and attractive way to join limbs onto soft toys, and enables them to move – so Finnegan here can reach out for a cooling beverage! But omit the buttons if you are making him for a small child, as they are a potential choking hazard.

thirteen Iron fusible webbing to the wrong side of the white wool felt. Draw around the eye template twice onto the paper side and cut out. Peel away the paper from the eyes, position on Finnegan's face and press into place. Secure the eyes around the edge with blanket stitch using two strands of white embroidery thread (floss) (see page 107).

fourteen Draw around the pupil template twice onto the piece of black wool felt and cut out. Use fabric glue to stick the pupils in position on Finnegan's eyes and allow to dry. Using two strands of white embroidery thread (floss), create a double-wrap French knot in the centre of each pupil (see page 107).

fifteen Using the templates on page 118, mark the mouth and nostrils onto Finnegan's face and backstitch using four strands of black embroidery thread (floss) (see page 106).

sixteen From the red patterned fabric, draw around the shorts template once onto the fabric folded in half and cut out, to make two pieces. Place the two shorts pieces on top of each other, right sides together, and sew together along both crotch lines, taking a 6mm (¼in) seam. Open the shorts out and then refold them so that the two crotch seams lay against each other and the raw inner leg edges are now right sides together. Sew the inner legs together from the bottom of one leg up to the crotch and back down the other leg. Turn right side out and press.

Finnegan keeps his eye on the good things of life! Attached in position with iron-on fusible webbing, the white wool felt outer eye is then securely blanket-stitched to his head, while the black wool felt pupils are stuck on with fabric glue.

Finnegan's is a telling face – the chilled-out grin says it all. His head needs to be well filled out with stuffing to get a nice rounded effect and to maximize the easy smile.

To finish off Finnegan's beach shorts in speedy style, the legs are hemmed with two lines of topstitching – use a contrasting-coloured thread on your machine.

seventeen Hem the bottom edges of the shorts' legs by turning under 6mm (¼in) and then sewing with two lines of topstitching.

eighteen Turn under the top edge of the shorts by 6mm–1.25cm (¼–½in) and press. Topstitch the fold in place approximately 6mm (¼in) in from the folded edge. Place the shorts on Finnegan.

Tip

If the shorts are a little loose or you just wish to secure them, using your dollmaker's needle and a double length of thread, make a small stitch in the centre front of the shorts (over your topstitching), then insert the needle through the body and out through the centre back of the shorts. Make a stitch through the shorts, then reverse the process back through to the front of the shorts. Repeat a few times to ensure a strong attachment. Tie off and sink the knot into the body (see page 109).

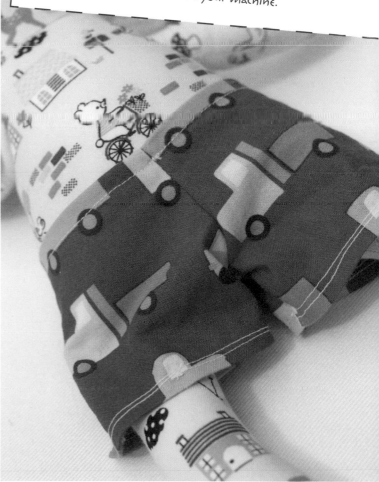

Tools and Techniques

Basic tool kit

Make sure you have the following before you embark on making any of the toys in the book – all the essentials specified here are basic items of a sewing kit.

Template plastic

This is the best material for tracing off or copying the templates for the toys (provided on pages 116–125) and making your own templates to use, because you can see your fabric through it and therefore ensure correct placement. The markings from the printed templates can be transferred to the plastic templates with a permanent marker, or use a grey lead pencil if you are not concerned about permanence. You can then store your plastic templates and reuse them to make any number of toys. If you don't have any template plastic, you can cut the templates out of card instead.

Fabric markers

There are many different methods of marking your fabric and an array of products on the market. However, vanishing markers or tailor's chalk are the best options, to avoid making permanent marks on your toys. A light grey lead pencil is a handy substitute.

Rotary cutter, mat and ruler

These tools are designed to make the cutting of strips and squares a simple and accurate procedure. Although recommended, they are not essential items and you can use a tape measure, ruler and scissors instead.

Sewing thread

It's very important to use strong thread when sewing toys that are going to be stuffed. Therefore, always choose a good-quality polyester thread for all machine sewing, as this will ensure strong seams and make your soft toys more durable.

Fusible webbing

This widely available iron-on material is used to adhere all the appliqué pieces, such as facial features, to the toys. Be sure to check the manufacturer's instructions for your specific product before using.

Embroidery thread (floss)

You will need six-strand embroidery thread (floss) for embroidering the toys' facial features and for the hand blanket-stitched appliqué details.

Embroidery needles

A size 10 embroidery needle is recommended for hand embroidery stitching, appliqué and closing the turning gaps on your toys.

Dollmaker's needles

These are extra-long needles used for button jointing (see page 114).

Toy filling

Choose a good-quality polyester toy filling for stuffing your toys – see page 110 for advice on what to look for.

Light box

A light box is the most effective way of tracing details onto fabric. These can be very useful for placing as well as drawing on stitching lines. However, if you don't have a light box and would rather not invest in one, a sunny window can be just as effective. Place your templates and/or fabric against a light window and tape to the window with masking tape. The window should give enough light to see through your layers and make any markings.

Other essentials

- Sewing machine
- Good-quality, sharp sewing scissors
- Dressmaker's pins
- Tacking thread and sewing needles
- Turning/stuffing tools: wooden skewer and paintbrush tool
- Iron and ironing board

Choosing fabric

All the main fabrics used in the creation of the soft toys in this book are 100% cotton patchwork fabrics. It's important that you always use quality cotton fabrics for making your toys in order to achieve equally good results. Some of the toy projects use wool felt, such as for facial features. Again, make sure that you purchase a quality product that has a percentage of wool content, such as those available from patchwork suppliers, rather than one that is 100% synthetic.

Most patchwork fabric is 102–112cm (40–44in) wide and this width is allowed for in the fabric requirements specified in the 'you will need' listings for each toy. If you are using narrower fabrics, you may need to make adjustments accordingly.

Deciding on your choice of fabrics for your toys is as important as neat sewing or professional stuffing, and it's essential to devote enough time to looking at different combinations of colours and patterns. Which fabrics you select will always be a personal decision, reflecting your own individual taste, but the following guidelines will help you to make the most effective choices and achieve eye-catching results.

Creative contrasts

For a bold impact, go for unconventional combinations of fabrics for maximum contrast, such as mixing geometrics with florals or pastels with bright colours. Just remember to build your composition around some degree of colour continuity to link the disparate fabrics and then experiment with different mixes to a get a pleasing end result.

Pushing the boundaries

Making soft toys gives you the opportunity to take risks with your fabric choices and to move beyond your usual comfort zone. Remember that you are not making an heirloom quilt here, so you have the freedom to be experimental and 'play'. Abandon the rules and go with your first instinct – there are no wrong choices, and if your favoured combination of fabrics makes you happy, that's the perfect outcome!

Colour combos

If a project requires multiple fabrics, make sure that each fabric has a colour in common with at least one or two of the other fabrics you are combining. If you choose a range of fabrics that all coordinate with each other, the end result is liable to be too predictable and bland-looking.

Mixing scale and pattern

Try mixing small-scale patterned fabrics with large- and medium-scale prints, as well as spots, stripes and checks. This gives greater emphasis to the different elements, allowing each fabric to stand out from the other.

Hand sewing

The following basic stitches are used in the making of the toys featured in the book, with the diagrams demonstrating how to work the stitches.

Ladder stitch

This stitch is used to sew turning gaps closed and also to attach parts to stuffed toys, such as Mabelle's snout pictured here.

Backstitch

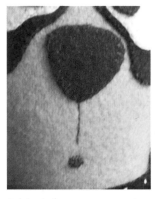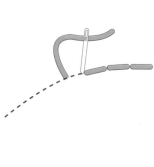

Backstitch creates a continuous line of stitching, so it's ideal for defining shapes. It's used here to add the expressive line running down from Lou-Lou's nose.

Chain stitch

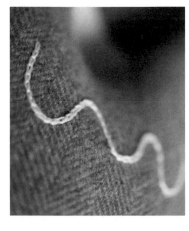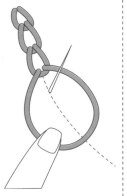

Chain stitch is great for creating thicker lines, and therefore perfect for embroidering Harry's long, wiggly mouth, as shown here.

Running stitch

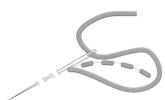

This simple stitch is used to embroider circles for Tilly's cheeks. It's also sewn along the edges of fabric, without securing the thread end, and the thread pulled up to gather it, such as for the waist and leg bottoms of Tilly's pantaloons.

French knot

The double-wrap French knot creates a prominent raised dot, which is used for adding a centre to some of the toys' pupils, as in Finnegan's case shown here.

Cross stitch

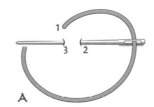

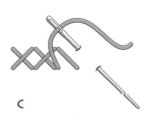

Cross stitch is used as an alternative to the French knot to add a 'twinkling' centre to some of the toys' pupils, for example Pearl's as pictured here.

Satin stitch

First backstitch around the outside edge of the shape and then satin stitch over the stitching (see diagrams).

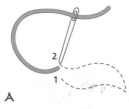

Satin stitch is useful for filling in small areas with embroidery, such as eyes and Alvin's tongue, as shown here.

Blanket stitch

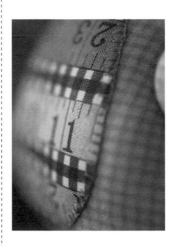

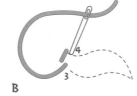

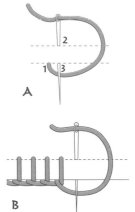

This edging stitch is used to secure appliquéd fabric pieces, such as outer eyes and pupils, as well as Preston's tummy patch, where it adds a smart finishing touch.

Machine sewing

For all sewing of the body pieces for the toys, set the stitch length on your sewing machine to 1.5mm (¹⁄₁₆in) and use good-quality strong polyester thread. For the sewing of clothing, set the stitch length to 2.5mm (³⁄₃₂in).

Where machine appliquéing is required, set your sewing machine to blanket stitch where possible. If your machine doesn't have blanket stitch, use a zigzag stitch instead.

Lock your stitching by starting and ending all machine sewing with a few reverse stitches. This ensures that the seam won't split when you are turning and stuffing your soft toys.

Some of the toy body pieces require stitching along the marked outline before cutting out, while others will have a 6mm (¼in) seam allowance allowed in the pattern pieces. Therefore, make sure that you read the full instructions for making each toy before you begin.

Sinking knots

You may be required to attach appliqué pieces or limbs, or add stitching, after a toy has been completed. This is when you want to avoid any knots being visible where you start and end your stitching by sinking them, to ensure a neat finish.

ONE Thread your needle with the specified number of strands of thread. Tie a knot in the end as usual – use a double knot if using two strands of thread or, as a general guideline, make sure it's about the same width as your needle. Insert the needle into your toy a short distance away from where you want to start your stitching, then bring the needle tip out at the exact place you want to begin.

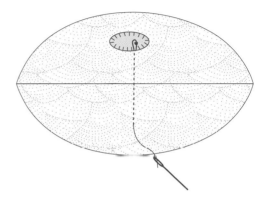

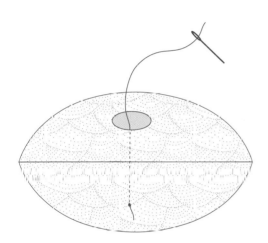

two Pull the thread through and the knot will catch at your point of entry. Grab the thread close to its exit point and give it a quick short tug. This will cause the knot to pop through the weave of your fabric and sink inside the toy. Make sure you don't tug too hard or your knot may be pulled through both layers of fabric.

three Complete the sewing required on your toy. When you are ready to take your last stitch, tie a knot the same width as before close to the base of your thread. Make your last stitch, taking the needle through to the same area where you first entered, on the back of the toy if possible. Again, your thread will snag when the knot reaches the fabric. Tug the thread to sink this knot into the toy. Cut the thread right at the fabric, which will also sink into the toy.

Tying a reef (square) knot

It's important to tie thread in a proper double knot, known as a reef or square knot, as shown below, to make sure that it doesn't come undone.

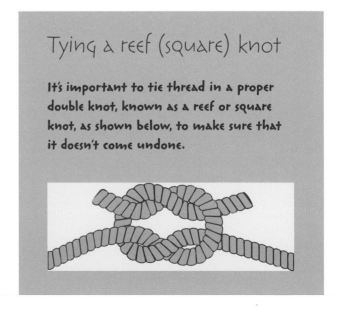

Stuffing

It's essential to stuff your toys very firmly, and you will be surprised at how much filling they need.
Bear in mind that you will have sewn the seams with small stitches using strong polyester thread
and therefore they will be robust enough to withstand a large amount of stuffing. So when you
think that your toy is fully stuffed, keep on stuffing! And don't feel scared to use large wads of filling,
as this will give your toy more structure.

Choosing toy filling

Always use a good-quality toy filling when making soft
toys. Some fillings can create lumps inside your toys, giving
them a rough and uneven finish. To check a filling for quality,
take a small handful of the filling and roll it gently into a ball
between your palms. If the filling remains in a tight ball, it
will create lumps, but if it springs back, it's ideal to use.

Stuffing/turning tools

Some of the most effective tools for stuffing your toys are
standard household items, so there is no need to invest in
expensive stuffing tools to get the perfect results. There are
two such items that are unrivalled for the task of stuffing:

WOODEN SKEWER
When turning (see opposite) and stuffing very small pieces,
use a wooden skewer, which you will find sold in bulk packs
at supermarkets. Be careful to use the blunt end of the stick
only – the pointed end is liable to break your seams.

PAINTBRUSH TOOL
A widely available, inexpensive round wooden paintbrush
makes a great double-sided turning/stuffing tool. The
smooth handle of the paintbrush is perfect for turning
your soft toy pieces and smoothing out the seams prior to
stuffing, while the bristle end becomes the ideal stuffing
tool with just a little modification. Trim the bristles to 6mm–
1.25cm (¼– ½in) long. Play with the remaining bristles using
your fingers and rub them against a hard surface until you
have messed them up thoroughly so that they are nice and
shaggy. Shaggy bristles are desirable as they will grip onto

your filling firmly and stay adhered, allowing you to easily
manoeuvre it into your toy. They will also enable you to
position the filling where you want it and to keep stuffing it
right to the end of the toy pieces until they are super-firm.

Stuffing legs of all-in-one toys

When the legs are an integral part of the template for the
whole toy, as with Darcy the Dinosaur (pages 54–59),
Gerbera the Giraffe (pages 68–75) and Polly the Pig (pages
84–91), you can sometimes have trouble filling the legs
adequately to ensure that they hold the weight of the toy
without buckling. Start by stuffing the legs with decent-
sized wads of filling and then continue to stuff the rest of
your toy. When you think you have almost completely
stuffed the toy, use your paintbrush tool to manoeuvre
more filling down the outside edges of the legs until the legs
feel firm and strong. The legs may also buckle if there is not
enough filling between the tops of the legs and the body.

Turning small pieces

Sometimes you may be required to sew, turn and stuff very small or narrow pieces.
This can be quite fiddly and frustrating, but here is a handy technique to make the task
that much easier. You will need a drinking straw – one that's a little sturdier than the standard
bulk pack variety, such as those you get from fast food outlets. A reusable plastic straw is perfect.

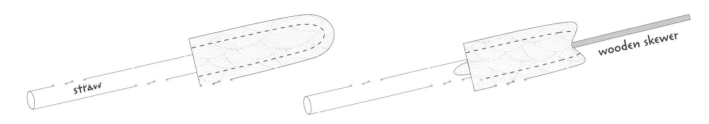

ONE Take the small body piece that requires stuffing between your two fingers and twist the fabric against itself to open it up. Slide the small fabric piece over the end of your straw.

two Using the blunt end of your wooden skewer, push the sewn end of the fabric piece back into the covered end of the straw.

three Keep pushing the fabric piece into the straw so that it turns the piece right side out. Continue pushing the fabric piece through to the other end of the straw.

Sewing turning gaps closed

Some turning gaps may be visible on your completed toy and therefore it's important that the closure is as neat as possible.

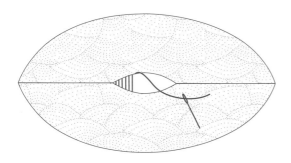

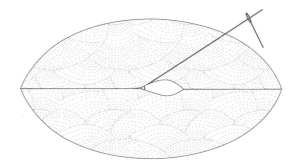

ONE Using two strands of strong polyester thread, sink your knot into the toy, as instructed on page 109, and start your stitching at one end of the gap. Use ladder stitch (see diagram on page 106) to sew the two edges closed.

two Once you have ladder stitched approximately 1.25cm (½in) of the gap, pull the thread slowly but firmly away from the stitching towards the remainder of the gap in order to bring the two edges together.

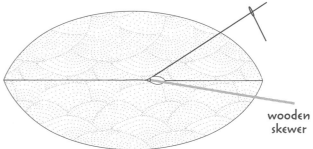

wooden skewer

three Continue to sew up the gap in the same way, pulling the fabric edges together after each 1.25cm (½in) has been stitched. Once you have only 1.25cm (½in) of your gap left to stitch, stuff a little more filling into the area just stitched to avoid leaving a dimple in your toy. Do this by carefully using your wooden skewer to insert small pieces of filling.

four Once you are happy with your stuffing and there is no dimpling visible, sew the remainder of the gap closed. Sink a knot at the end to secure your stitching.

Inserting legs

It's easier to insert stuffed legs into the body of your toy before stuffing the body section.

ONE To do this, fold the bottom edge of the body in by 6mm (¼in) and press in place.

two Take the stuffed legs and, ensuring that they are facing the correct way, tack (baste) the top raw edges in place between the two folded edges of the body front and body back. Position the left leg at the left side of the body and the right leg at the right side so that there is a gap between the two legs. Topstitch the legs in place through all the layers with your sewing machine, leaving the gap between the legs open for stuffing. Now you will be able to fill the head/body section firmly through the gap between the legs without the filling escaping. When the body is fully stuffed, ladder stitch the gap closed (see opposite).

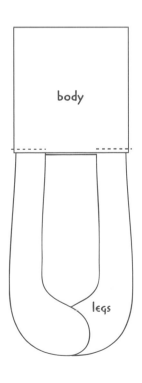

body

legs

Button jointing

This technique is a quick, easy and effective way of attaching limbs to your soft toy creations. One of the great benefits of button jointing is that it makes the limbs movable while remaining extremely secure. It also eliminates the need for a lot of intricate hand sewing and can give an added visual appeal to your toys if you choose decorative, complementary-coloured buttons.

one To attach limbs using the button-jointing method, take your long dollmaker's needle (see page 103) and thread it with a long length of six-strand embroidery thread (floss) in a colour to match your buttons. Tie a double knot in the end of your length of thread and trim close to the knot.

two Start by threading the needle through one side seam of the toy's body at the desired location, right through the body and out the other side seam at the same limb level.

three Now thread the needle through one of the limbs, approximately 1.75cm (¾in) down from the top limb edge, through one of your buttons and then back through all the layers again to the other side. Here, thread the needle through your remaining limb and button (see diagram) and return again, through the body, to the other side.

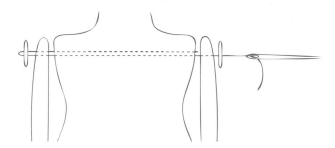

four Continue in the same way, taking the needle through all the layers a few times, until you have achieved a strong attachment. Tie off your thread and sink the knot into the limb (see page 109).

Alternative jointing method

If you are making your toy for a small child, it's important to avoid using any buttons, as they can be a choking hazard. In this case, simply make the join as in the button jointing technique left but without using buttons. Start by sinking a knot into one side of the toy's body, sew on the limbs, omitting the button, and then sink the thread knot into the body/limb again when you have finished stitching.

Attaching parts with ladder stitch

Sometimes the project instructions will require you to attach an item to the stuffed toy using ladder stitch. This method is usually used so that the attachment will either sit flat against or protrude from the stuffed toy. Follow the ladder stitch diagram on page 106, but make one stitch in the edge of the attachment, then make the next stitch in the body of the toy. The ladder stitches need to be sewn into the body following the shape of the attachment so that the latter retains its shape.

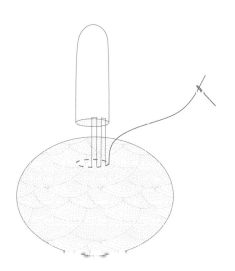

Painting on fabric

This technique is used to create Tilly the Doll's shoes (see page 15). You will need acrylic folk art paint and a flat-bristled paintbrush. First mark the outline of the area to be painted on the fabric with a light grey lead pencil. Use the flat edge of the paintbrush bristles to guide the paint, undiluted, along the drawn line, then fill in the rest of the area with even paint strokes. Allow to dry naturally or use a hair dryer to speed up the process. Paint over the painted area with a water-based acrylic varnish. Choose a gloss varnish to create the resemblance of patent leather, or use matt varnish to give the effect of suede.

Templates

ENLARGE ALL TEMPLATES BY 200%

Alvin the alien
(pages 76–83)

body

upper eye pupil

middle outer eye

upper outer eye

middle eye pupil

leave open

arm

leave open

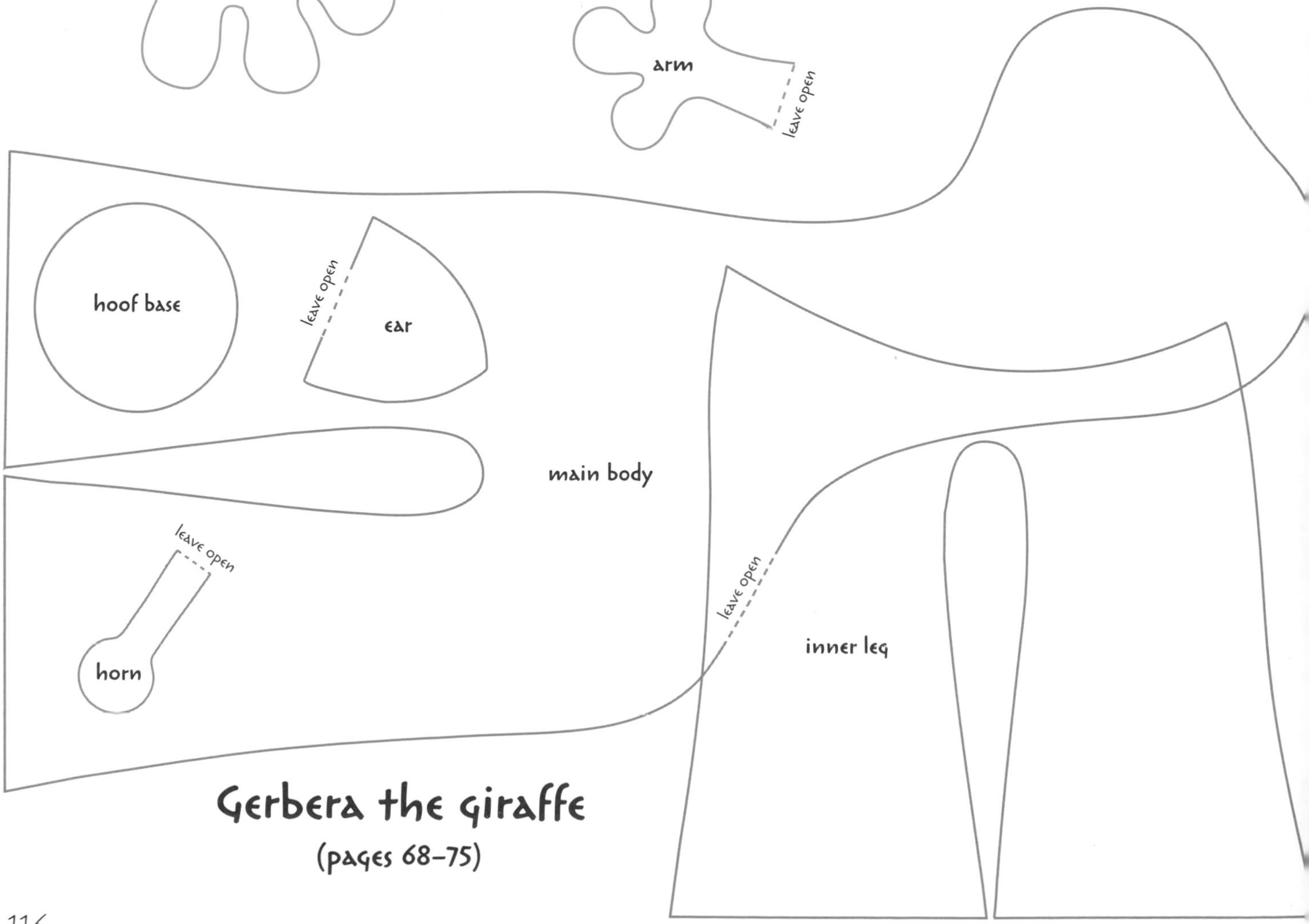

hoof base

leave open

ear

main body

horn

leave open

leave open

inner leg

Gerbera the giraffe
(pages 68–75)

Darcy the dinosaur
(pages 54–59)

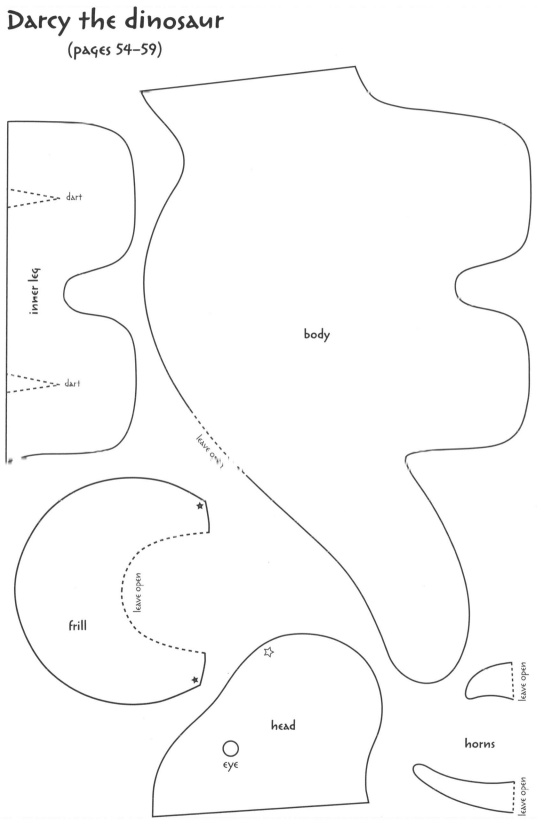

inner leg

dart

dart

leave open

body

frill

leave open

leave open

head

eye

horns

leave open

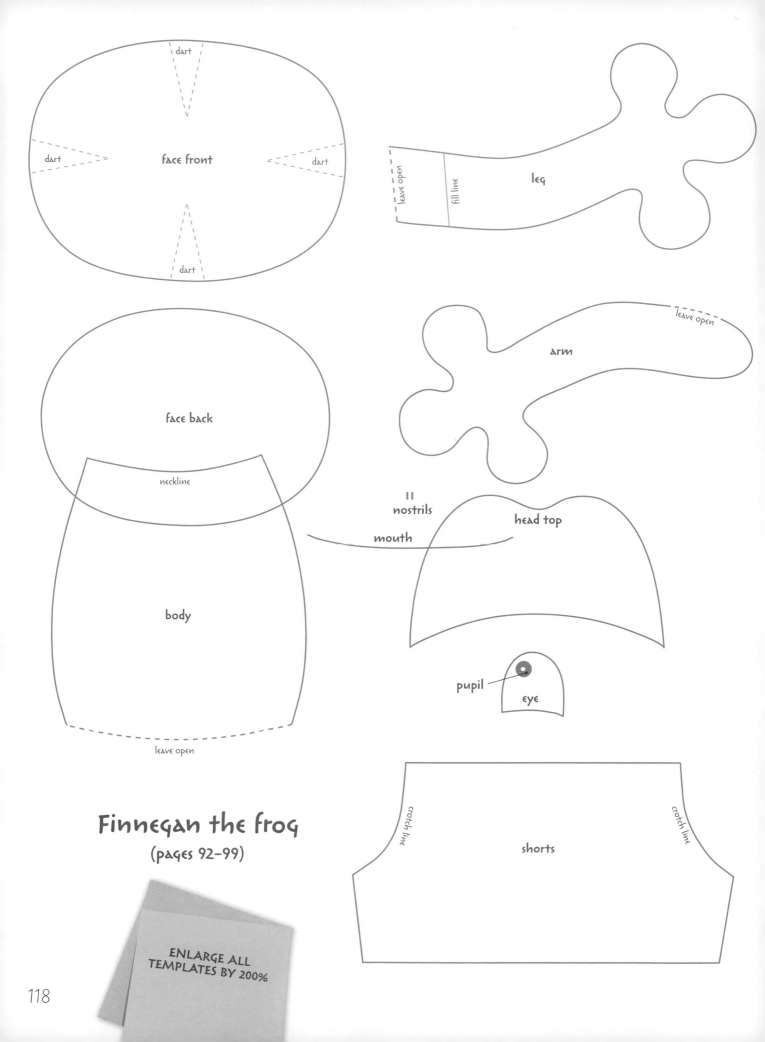

face front

dart

dart | dart

dart

leg

leave open | fill line

face back

neckline

arm

leave open

body

nostrils

mouth

head top

pupil

eye

leave open

Finnegan the frog
(pages 92–99)

ENLARGE ALL TEMPLATES BY 200%

shorts

crotch line

crotch line

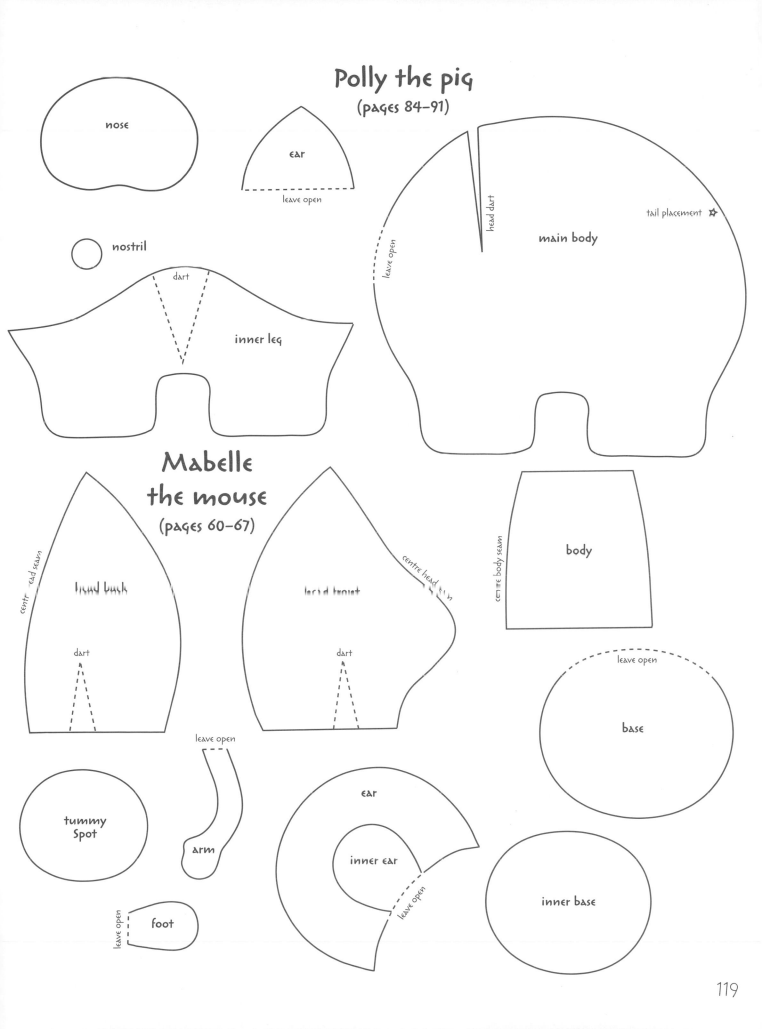

Polly the pig
(pages 84–91)

nose

ear

leave open

nostril

dart

inner leg

head dart

leave open

main body

tail placement ✿

Mabelle
the mouse
(pages 60–67)

centre head seam

head back

head front

centre head seam

centre body seam

body

dart

dart

leave open

base

tummy
Spot

leave open

arm

ear

inner ear

inner base

leave open

leave open

foot

leave open

119

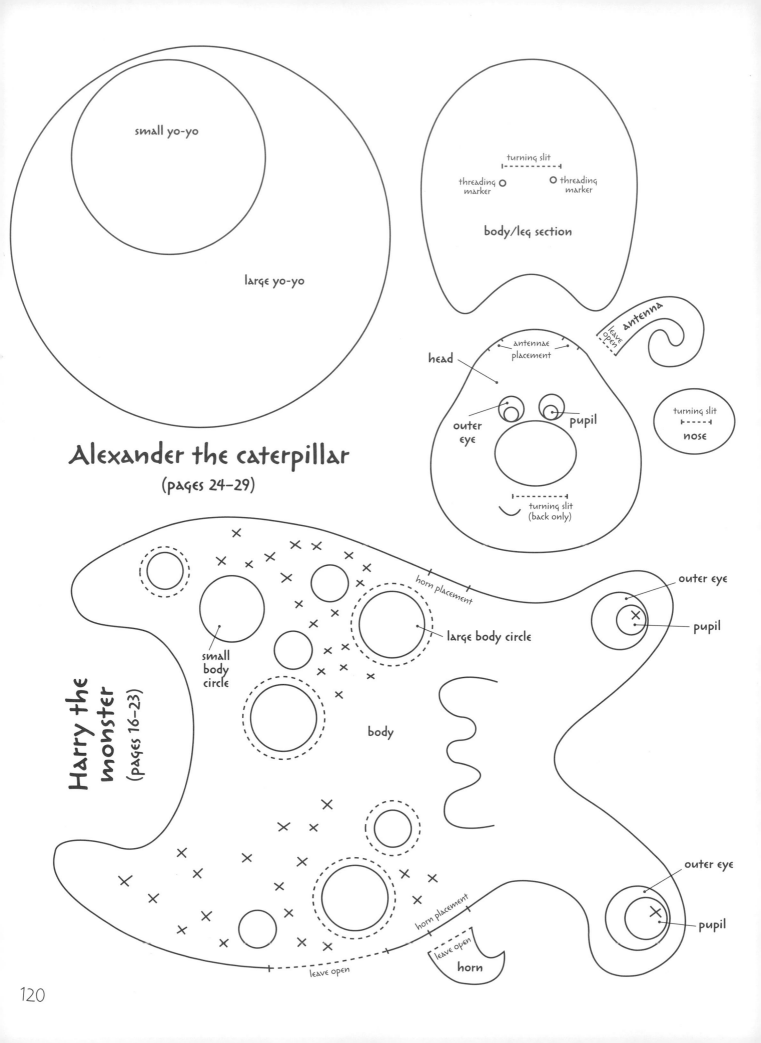

small yo-yo

large yo-yo

turning slit

threading marker ○   ○ threading marker

body/leg section

leave open

antenna

head

antennae placement

outer eye

pupil

turning slit

nose

turning slit (back only)

Alexander the caterpillar
(pages 24–29)

horn placement

outer eye

pupil

small body circle

large body circle

body

Harry the monster
(pages 16–23)

outer eye

pupil

horn placement

leave open

leave open

horn

120

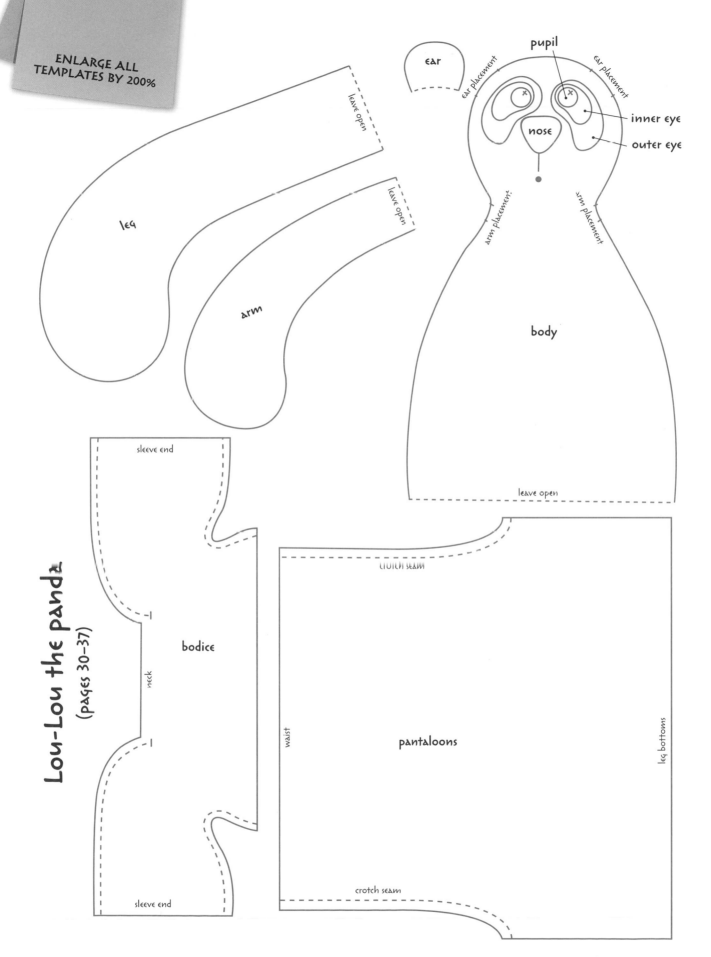

ENLARGE ALL
TEMPLATES BY 200%

ear

pupil

ear placement

ear placement

inner eye

nose

outer eye

leave open

leg

leave open

arm placement

arm placement

arm

body

leave open

sleeve end

crotch seam

Lou-Lou the panda
(pages 30–37)

bodice

neck

waist

pantaloons

leg bottoms

sleeve end

crotch seam

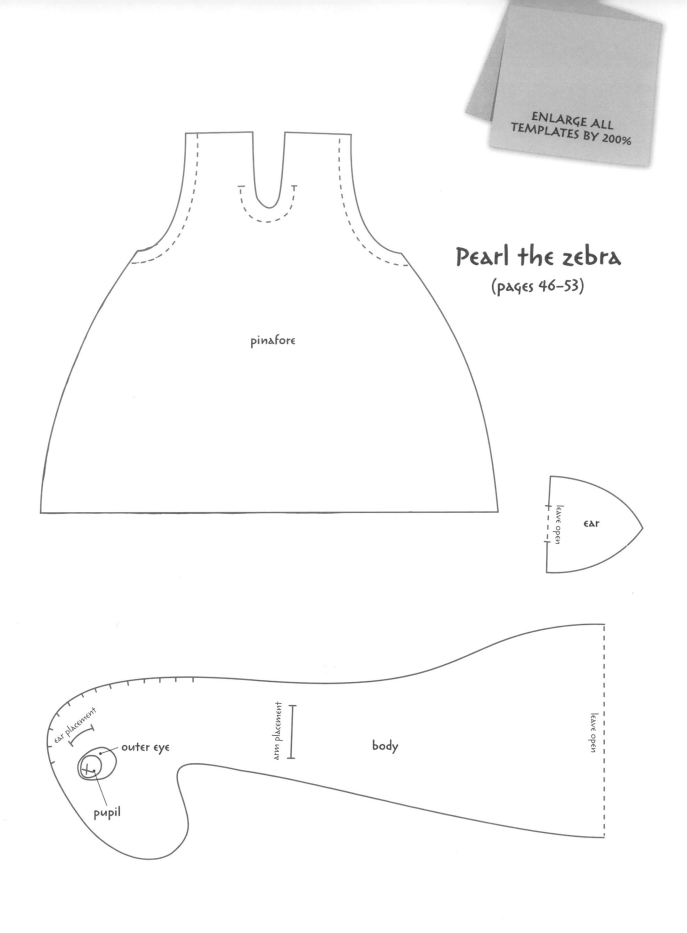

ENLARGE ALL
TEMPLATES BY 200%

Pearl the zebra
(pages 46–53)

pinafore

ear

leave open

ear placement

outer eye

pupil

arm placement

body

leave open

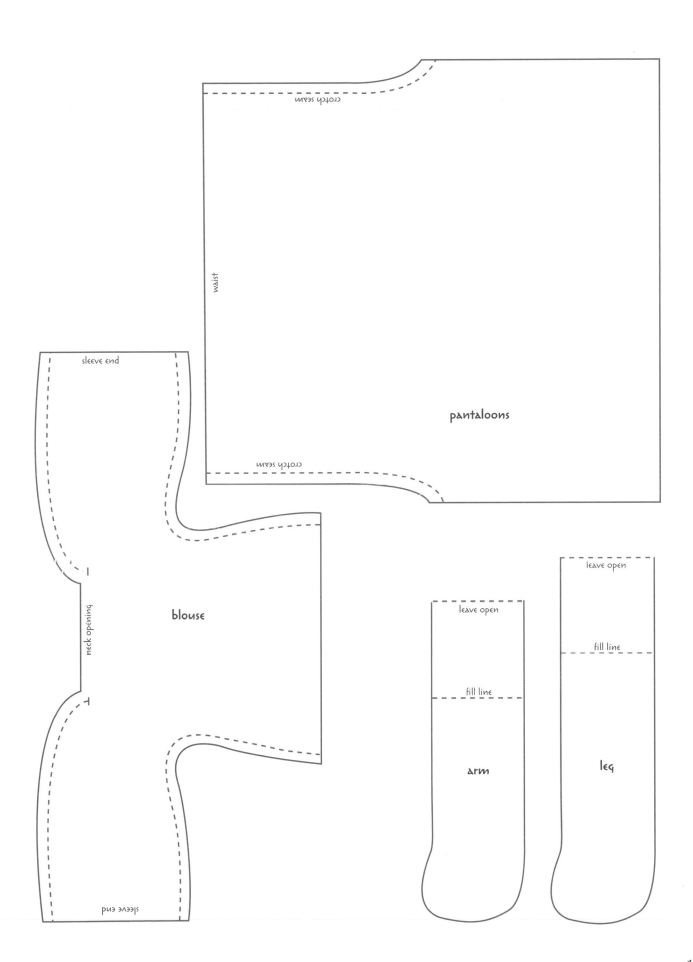

pantaloons

waist

crotch seam

crotch seam

sleeve end

blouse

neck opening

sleeve end

leave open

fill line

arm

leave open

fill line

leg

ENLARGE ALL
TEMPLATES BY 200%

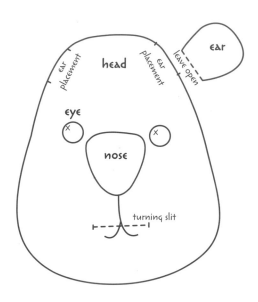

Preston the lion

(pages-38-45)

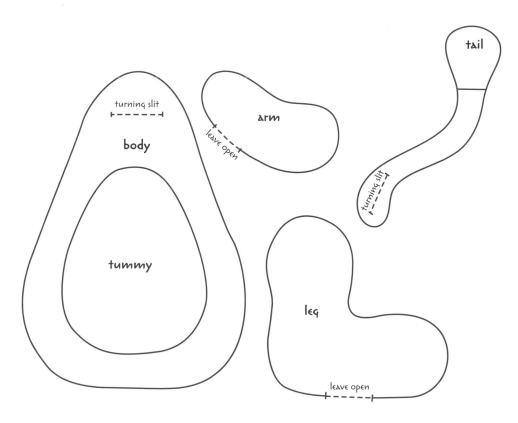

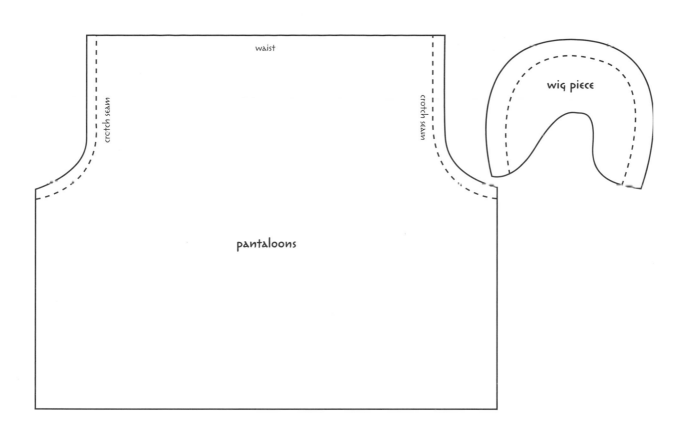

waist

crotch seam

crotch seam

wig piece

pantaloons

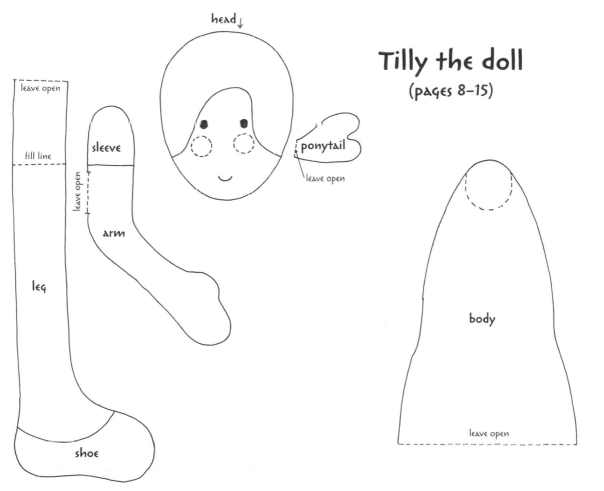

head ↓

Tilly the doll
(pages 8–15)

leave open

fill line

sleeve

leave open

arm

leave open

ponytail

leave open

leg

shoe

body

leave open

SUPPLIERS

UK

Cross Patch
Blaen Bran Farm, Velindre, Llandysul,
Carmarthenshire, SA44 5XT
Tel: +44 (0)1559 371018
www.cross-patch.co.uk

The Eternal Maker
41 Terminus Road, Chichester,
West Sussex, PO19 8TX
Tel: +44 (0)1243 788174
www.eternalmaker.com

The Fat Quarters
5 Chopwell Road, Blackhall Mill,
Newcastle upon Tyne, NE17 7TN
Tel: +44 (0)1207 565728
www.thefatquarters.co.uk

Fibrecrafts
Old Portsmouth Road,
Peasmarsh, Guildford,
Surrey, GU3 1LZ
Tel: +44 (0)1483 565800
www.fibrecrafts.com

Gone to Earth
12 Hill House Gardens,
Stanwick, Wellingborough,
Northamptonshire, NN9 6QH
Tel: +44 (0)1933 623412
www.gonetoearth.co.uk

Hulu Crafts
Sentinel House, Poundwell,
Modbury, Devon, PL21 0XX
Tel: +44 (0)1548 831911
www.hulucrafts.co.uk

USA

Connecting Threads
13118 NE 4th Street,
Vancouver, WA 98684
Tel: +1 800 574 6454
www.connectingthreads.com

Craft Connection
21055 Front Street, PO Box 1088,
Onley, VA 23418
Tel: +1 888 204 4050
www.craftconn.com

Hancocks of Paducah
3841 Hinkleville Road,
Paducah, KY 42001
Tel: +1 800 845 8723
www.hancocks-paducah.com

JoAnn Stores Inc
5555 Darrow Road, Hudson,
OH 44236
Tel: +1 888 739 4120
www.joann.com

MMIJA
4865 West Andrew Johnson Hwy,
Morristown, TN 37814
Tel: +1 865 475 2200
www.mmija.com

Pine Needles Sewing Center
1000 Old Marion Rd NE,
Cedar Rapids, IA 52402
Tel: +1 319 373 0334
www.pineneedles.net

Pink Chalk Fabrics
9723 Coppertop Loop, Suite 205,
Bainbridge Island, WA 98110
Tel: +1 888 894 0658
www.pinkchalkfabrics.com

AUSTRALIA

Ballarat Patchwork
54 Victoria Street, Ballarat, VIC 3350
Tel: +61 (0)3 5332 6722
www.ballaratpatchwork.com.au

Creative Abundance
PO Box 7244, Upper Ferntree Gully,
VIC 3156
Tel: +61 (0)3 9753 5459
www.creativeabundance.com.au
*Wholesale supplier of Melly & Me
sewing patterns*

Fabric Patch
288 Yandina Coolum Rd,
Coolum Beach, QLD 4573
Tel: +61 (0)7 5446 3695
www.fabricpatch.com.au

Funky Fabrix
Shop 5/40 Blackwood Street,
Mitchelton, QLD 4503
Tel: +61 (0)4 3501 2356
www.funkyfabrix.com.au

The Patchwork Angel
343 Mons Road, Forest Glen,
Sunshine Coast, QLD 4556
Tel: +61 (0)7 5477 0700
www.patchworkangel.com.au

Raspberry Hill Fabrics
Diamond Creek, VIC 3089
Tel: +61 (0)3 9438 1239
www.raspberryhillfabrics.com.au

Under the Mulberry Tree
Po Box 429, Ferntree Gully BC,
VIC 3156
Tel: +61 (0)4 3791 8186
www.underthemulberrytree.com

ABOUT THE AUTHORS

Rosalie Quinlan has been passionate about craft and sewing for most of her life. She began designing her own patterns for dolls, bags and quilts 14 years ago under the label Rosalie Quinlan Design, and went on to teach sewing throughout Australia and also internationally. In 2006, Rosalie teamed up with her sister, Melanie Hurlston, to set up a second design label, Melly & Me, which gave her the opportunity to explore fun and zany designs rather than more traditional work. Rosalie is also a regular contributor to various Australian and international quilting magazines, and in 2009 she embarked on designing textiles for the Japanese company Lecien, recently releasing her second range of fabric titled 'Sweet Broderie'.

Melanie Hurlston is a pattern designer based in Melbourne, Australia. Melly's adventures in sewing began six years ago when she discovered, as an at-home mother, that she still had the desire to be creative and productive. Her passion for sewing quickly grew after her sister, Rosalie Quinlan, encouraged her to give it a try, and only 12 months after starting to sew she began designing under the pattern label Melly & Me. Melly's goal was to develop a range of contemporary sewing patterns that included bright and quirky toys, wearable purses and lively, modern quilts. Her aim is to design items that are original, fun and achievable in a day, as well as being completely usable in everyday life. In 2010 Melly launched a second design label, Sew Little, which includes patterns that are aimed at the baby market. The same year also saw Melly launch her first two fabric collections – 'Little Menagerie' for Windham Fabrics and 'Where the Wind Blows' for Creative Abundance. Melly draws her inspiration from her two young children, childhood memories and her love of colour.

Melly & Me
www.mellyandme.typepad.com
mellyandme@optusnet.com

Rosalie Quinlan Designs
www.rosaliequinlandesigns.typepad.com

ACKNOWLEDGMENTS

We wish to thank our parents, Nel and Jacques, for their continued support and encouragement, and especially for providing a creative environment during our childhood.

We would love to thank all of the team at D&C for making this book a reality and bringing our creations to life.

We also thank our families for always supporting and encouraging our dreams.
Last but not least, we would like to thank all of the wonderful women (and sometimes men) who have bought our patterns, attended our classes and followed our journey so far.

Index